Native Americans

VOLUME 10

TOLTEC–ZUNI

GROLIER
EDUCATIONAL

About this book

Thousands of years ago groups of hunter-gatherers from Asia began crossing the Bering Strait land bridge, which temporarily linked Siberia and Alaska. These earliest American settlers found a land of extreme environmental contrasts. Over the centuries the groups—ancestors of Native Americans—settled throughout North and South America, forming tribes and creating cultures and lifestyles that were influenced by their local environment. As in all parts of the world, conflicts emerged between the different tribes, but it was not until the arrival of Europeans in the late 15th and early 16th centuries that the survival of all Native Americans began to be threatened. Warfare, disease, and first European then American expansion combined to rid Native Americans of their homeland and, in most cases, their way of life. In the process whole tribes were wiped out, but many have survived. And for those that have, modern life has brought new challenges, cultural and political, that nonnative Americans are beginning to be made aware of.

There are 10 volumes in this set profiling all of the major Native-American groups, the history of their lives in each region, and background anthropology, archaeology, and other topics key to understanding Native Americans. Each volume contains entries ranging from important Native-American events and figures to wide-ranging beliefs and customs, an A–Z of some 90 tribes, and an index that covers the whole set. Also, each entry is fully illustrated with pictures, photographs, or maps and concludes with a list of cross-references to other entries in the set. This means readers can refer to each volume as a series of stories or cross-reference from one volume to another, following a subject that particularly interests them.

Published 2000 by Grolier Educational
Sherman Turnpike
Danbury, Connecticut 06816

Set ISBN: 0-7172-9395-5
Volume ISBN: 0-7172-9405-6

Cover picture: Peter Newark Historical Pictures

For information address the publisher:
Grolier Educational, Sherman Turnpike, Danbury, Connecticut 06816

Library of Congress Cataloging-in-Publication Data
Native Americans
p.cm.—Includes index.—Contents: v.1. Acoma–basketry—v.2. Bat cave–children—v.3. Chinook–education—v.4. El Tajín–Huron—v.5. Indian claims commission–longhouse religion—v.6. Mangas Coloradas–Muskogean speakers—v.7. Naskapi–Pontiac's war—v.8. Population density–Sauk and Fox—v.9. Scalping–tobacco—v.10. Toltec–Zuni.
1. Indians of North America Encyclopedia. Juvenile. [1. Indians of North America Encyclopedia.]
E76.2.N375 1999 99-28319
970.004'97'003—dc21 CIP

For Brown Partworks Ltd
Consultant: Norman Bancroft Hunt
Managing Editor: Dawn Titmus
Project Editor: Lee Stacy
Art Director: Bradley Davis
Designer: Paul Griffin
Text Editors: Robert Dimery, Peter Harrison, Lol Henderson, and Patrick Newman
Picture Research: Susannah Jayes and Rebecca Watson
Index: Kay Ollerenshaw
Maps: William Lebihan

Printed in Singapore

CONTENTS

Toltec	4
Tomahawk	7
Totemism	8
Totem Pole	10
Trade	12
Trail of Tears	15
Travois	17
Treaties	19
Tsimshian	23
Tula	27
Upper Missouri Tribes	28
Urban Life	32
Uto-Aztecan	34
Uxmal	35
Vision Quest	36
Wagon Trails	38
Wampum	40
War Costumes	41
War of 1812	43
Warriors	45
Warrior Societies	48
Water Rights	50
Women	52
Woodland	56
Wounded Knee	59
Wovoka	61
Zuni	62
A–Z of Native-American Tribes	65
Further Reading	71
Set Index	72
Acknowledgments	80

Toltec

LEFT: These giant stone warriors date from the time of the Toltec empire. They stand on the top of a pyramid in Tula.

The Toltec were a mixture of peoples who migrated north after the decline of the great city of Teotihuacan in southern Mexico about A.D. 950. They settled in north, northwest, and central Mexico, establishing their capital at Tollan (Tula), about 250 miles (400 km) north of present-day Mexico City. The Toltec empire lasted for 270 years. Its influence spread out across the Yucatán Peninsula and over Mesoamerica (the area from central Mexico to Nicaragua) to Honduras.

History of Tula

Tula was built around a highland lake bed (the name means "place of reeds"). The ruins of its ceremonial center and the outlying housing districts indicate that Tula was a prosperous place. Ancient texts refer to buildings full of offerings (turquoise, shells, and feathers) brought from peoples over whom the Toltec ruled. Little is known about the early period of Tula's history apart from the existence of a cult of the god Quetzalcoatl and the presence of many skilled artisans.

The references to Quetzalcoatl can be confusing, since it was also the name of one of the Toltec's first leaders. According to an ancient text called the *Annals of Cuauhitlan*, a warrior called Mixcoatl had a son named Ce Acatl Topiltzin, who was also known as Quetzalcoatl. He was named after the Toltec god because he was wise and peaceable.

Quetzalcoatl helped found Tula, but followers of the warrior god Tezcatlipoca soon rose up and drove him out of the city. According to one legend, Quetzalcoatl reached the shores of the Gulf of Mexico, where he set himself on fire and became the Morning Star. He vowed to return one day to reclaim his kingdom.

This prophecy could explain why Hernando Cortés found it easy to overrun the Aztec empire. The Aztecs admired the Toltec and claimed Quetzalcoatl as an Aztec god. Cortés resembled images of Quetzalcoatl, and the appearance of a Spanish force on the Yucatán Peninsula in 1519 was taken by many Aztecs to mark the return of the god. Some historians have found little evidence for the prophecy in oral traditions, however, and suggest that it was added after the Spanish invasion.

Toltec and Maya

There is evidence from Mayan texts that a band of Toltec warriors seized the Mayan city of Chitchén Itzá soon after the foundation of Tula, forming a Toltec–Maya state. One of the buildings in Chitchén Itzá, the Temple of the Warriors, closely resembles the main temple at present-day Tula. The Castillo (or Quetzalcoatl) pyramid and ball court (the largest in Mesoamerica) are also

BELOW: The Pyramid of the Sun, shown here, is one of the largest artificial mounds in America. It was part of the ancient Toltec city of Teotihuacan. Scholars believe that although the Toltec did not build the pyramid, they used it in their ceremonies.

Fact File

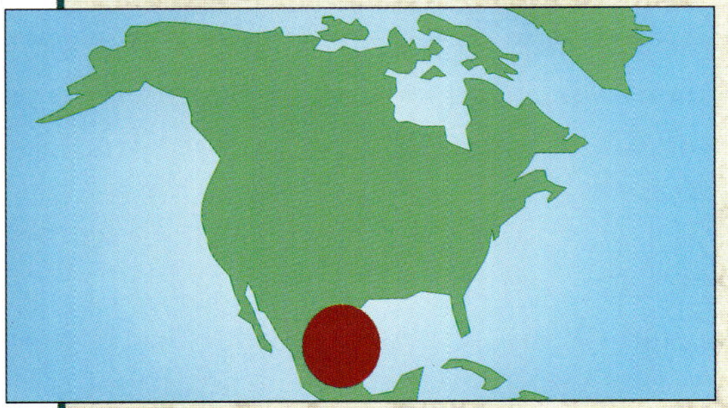

The influence of the Toltec empire spread across Mesoamerica.

LANGUAGE:	*Nahuatl*
AREA:	*Central Mexico*
POPULATION:	*Approximately 60,000 in Tula about A.D. 1000*
HOUSING:	*Stone houses*
EUROPEAN CONTACT:	*None*
NEIGHBORS:	*Chichimec, Mixtec, and Tononca*
LIFESTYLE:	*Farmers and warriors*
FOOD:	*Corn, beans, and squash*
CRAFTS:	*Sculptures, featherwork, and jewelry (gold and precious stones)*

Toltec-influenced. Within two centuries Chitchén Itzá was in ruins, and many Toltec moved to highland Guatemala. According to the *Popul Vuh*, a Mayan text discovered in the 18th century, these Toltec were the ancestors of the Quiche Maya.

The height of the Toltec empire was during the 11th and 12th centuries, when the Toltec ruled much of central Mexico. But about 1170 Tula was attacked by fierce nomads (probably Chichimec), and the great city was reduced to ruins.

Later the Aztecs viewed the Toltec empire as a golden age of peace and prosperity. When the Aztec leader Itzcoatl destroyed the old Aztec histories in 1428, he rewrote the Aztec genealogy (line of descent) to show them as the true heirs of the Toltec. Being a Toltec became identified with being "civilized."

Art and Architecture

There are very few written records to tell us about the Toltec. Most of what we know about these people comes from their art and architecture, which are dominated by images of warfare.

The ruins of Tula include the Burned Palace, two ball courts, and three stepped pyramid temples. The most important ruin (known as Temple B by archaeologists) is characterized by several colossal columns over 15 feet (4.5 m) high that once supported a roof. They are made from four sections of basalt (volcanic rock) pegged together and feature carvings of warrior figures.

Images around the temple include processions of jaguars and coyotes, eagles tearing at human hearts, and effigies (likenesses) of Quetzalcoatl. Dotted around the temple and elsewhere in the ruins are the chacmools—reclining figures with bowls on their chests. These bowls may have been designed to receive sacrificial offerings, though scholars do not believe the Toltec practiced human sacrifice on the same scale as the Aztecs.

SEE ALSO:
- Aztecs
- Chitchén Itzá
- Cortés, Hernando
- Maya
- Pyramids
- Ritual
- Tula

Tomahawk

Along with bows and arrows, tomahawks, or "war hatchets," were traditional Native-American weapons. Tomahawks could be held in the hand and used as hatchets, or they could be thrown. The word "tomahawk" comes from an Algonquian word meaning "to knock down."

Different styles

Early tomahawks were made of stone. The head could be ax-shaped or round and was bound tightly to a strong wooden shaft with tough animal sinew. Native Americans later acquired iron and steel weapons from white traders and adapted them to make tomahawks. Metal tomahawk blades came in many shapes and sizes. Some were single hatchet-shaped blades, and some were pointed like spearheads. Others were double blades—for example, a hatchet on one side and a spike on the other.

Some wooden tomahawk handles were plain, while others were beautifully carved. Ceremonial tomahawks were sometimes adorned with feathers, perhaps those of an eagle. Sometimes tomahawks were made with hollow handles. These were tipped with an ax blade and a pipe bowl and could be used both as a weapon and as a pipe for smoking tobacco.

Native Americans also used a range of war clubs that looked similar to tomahawks. Gunstock clubs were made of a piece of wood that had been shaped like the butt of a rifle and had a metal blade sunk into one edge. Other wooden war clubs had a ball-shaped head into which a metal spike was set.

Some Native-American tribes ceremonially buried a tomahawk when they made peace with an enemy. This may have given rise to the well-known modern expression "to bury the hatchet."

SEE ALSO:
- Algonquian
- Bows and Arrows
- Feathers for Warriors
- Tobacco
- Trade
- Warrior Societies

RIGHT: The tomahawk-pipe in this picture was made by members of the Blackfoot tribe.

Totemism

Common among Native-American tribes, totemism is the belief that individuals can have a direct relationship with, or an ancestral link to, a particular spirit being—a totem. Sometimes several individuals in a clan (a group of families) share the same totem. The word "totem" comes from the Ojibway (Chippewa) word *ototeman*, meaning "relatives."

Native Americans frequently portray their totems in carvings and paintings as animals or birds. They also often include symbols of them in medicine bundles, in the form of fur or feathers.

The exact form of totems in North America varies widely from tribe to tribe and between cultural areas. At their simplest level they are thought of as personal guardians or helpers and are often associated with shamans (medicine men and women). Shamans' totems vary widely—each shaman has his or her own totem that he or she considers to be a source of power.

Warriors also used personal totems, but these tended to be more similar to each other and were usually related to animals that had skills a warrior needed or desired. A warrior might be

LEFT: The carved face at the top of this totem pole symbolizes a mythical spirit called Thunderbird. Made by Tlingit carvers, the pole stands in a state totem-pole park in Ketchikan, Alaska.

inspired by a turtle, for example, because turtles were supposed to be difficult to kill.

More elaborate totems are common in the Subarctic and Woodland regions. The Iroquois, for example, have bear clans and wolf clans to which many people belong. They believe they share a common bond with these animals and that clan members benefit from their virtues. They consider bears to be spiritually powerful and believe that bear-clan people can wield *orenda*, or supernatural power, most effectively. Wolves are renowned for their cooperative hunting skills and were once associated with warriors.

The best-known symbols of Native-American totemism are the carved totem poles put up by the tribes of the Northwest Coast. They are among the finest wood carvings produced by Native Americans. They represent both clan and family lineages (lines of descent) and depict, in animal form, spirits that are said to have helped the mythical founding ancestors of the clan and family. A family's totem pole may prominently show both the clan's totem—in the form of an eagle, for example—and the family totem, in the form of, say, a beaver.

Totemism today

Many Native Americans continue to place special importance on totems as a way of connecting with traditional values that have been handed down through the generations. In this way their totems serve as a reminder of tribal identity and pride, separate from the European traditions and beliefs that have been introduced to North America in the past 400 years.

Often, however, as among the Pueblo peoples of the Southwest, a belief in these ancient ancestral forces is combined with elements from Christianity. Symbols representing the powers of these ancestors frequently feature prominently during ceremonies held on the feast days of Christian saints.

ABOVE: The bear on this screen is the totem of the Brown Bear clan of a 19th-century Tlingit chief called Shakes. The hole at the base allows access to a sacred room in his house.

SEE ALSO:
- Clan
- Iroquois
- Masks
- Medicine
- Medicine Bundle
- Origin Myths
- Pueblo
- Shamanism
- Tlingit
- Totem Pole
- Warriors

Totem Pole

Most people know totem poles from their use in Hollywood movies as symbols of "Indianness." However, in reality the totem pole was used only among tribes of the Northwest Coast in British Columbia and southern Alaska. Indeed, the well-known free-standing carved pole is a late development. It dates only from the period after European trade contacts introduced metal woodworking tools.

Totem poles were originally elaborately carved and decorated supporting posts for houses. The poles bore symbols of an individual family's ancestry. In this sense they served a function similar to the coats of arms on the shields and pennants of knights in European history. Like the coats of arms, totem poles were a statement of family lineage (ancestry). They also often depicted animal spirits that were thought to have helped found a particular clan in the past.

Different uses

Over time Native Americans replaced their traditional woodcarving tools—which had shell blades—with more efficient iron tools obtained through trade with Europeans. The new tools enabled craftsmen to create larger totem poles.

Some poles served as ceremonial entrance posts to houses via an opening cut through their bases. Others were carved as free-standing posts to mark notable events. Totem poles might also have acted as memorials to individuals, with the carved crests depicting the various marriage ties between different families. Poles with a horizontal crossbar were used as burial posts—the deceased's coffin was placed on a ledge at the back of the pole.

Family prestige

Totem poles were often associated with family prestige. Putting up a new pole was accompanied by

BELOW: This Tlingit totem pole is in a state park in Ketchikan, Alaska. The bird at the top is an eagle.

ABOVE: The carving of a bear shown here is part of a Tlingit totem pole in a state park in Ketchikan, Alaska.

gigantic feasts and distributions of gifts (known as "potlatches") sponsored by the host family. The greater the honor being claimed, the larger the feasts and the more valuable the gifts. An extension of this was the putting up of ridicule posts, which one family would use to deliberately deride a rival family. The pole stood as a semipermanent marker of this mockery. The rival family could remove their shame only by "washing it away" through even greater and more lavish feasting and gift-giving.

Some totem poles were used as a welcoming post. Carved poles depicting mythical figures—such as the Bear Mother—with outstretched palms assured visitors that their hosts carried no weapons and, therefore, presented no threat to their safety. These figures were often placed at a beachhead where visitors would arrive by canoe.

Totem poles today

During the 19th and early 20th centuries many totem poles were cut down at the insistence of religious authorities who felt that the poles undermined their efforts to convert native populations to Christianity. Other poles were uprooted and taken to museums and totem-pole parks, where they stand today as a tribute to a supposed golden age of Northwest Coast woodcarving.

However, the woodcarving art has survived. Recently there has been a resurgence in pole-carving combined with a greater sense of awareness and pride in Native-American identity. Prestigious families and kin groups are once more sponsoring the activities of woodcarvers, often with the whole-hearted support of their communities.

SEE ALSO:
- Clan
- Death Customs
- Haida
- Homes
- Movies
- Northwest Coast
- Potlatch
- Totemism
- Trade

Trade

Native-American trade patterns were well established in North America before European contact. Trade routes crisscrossed the continent—Adena and Hopewell traders traveled from the Woodland region to virtually every corner of North America. Trade between the Southeast, Southwest, and Mexico flourished. Trading links between Florida and Cuba were also strong. Tribes of the Plateau traded materials from the Pacific Coast to Great Plains tribes. The Tlingit controlled trade routes into the interior from the coasts of northern British Columbia and southern Alaska and also made trade voyages in sea-going canoes south to California.

Most native trade was in goods and materials that could not be obtained locally and so were considered luxuries. Early European traders capitalized on exchanging European goods for native products, using preexisting native trade routes. White exploration of these trade routes contributed greatly to the opening of the so-called "wilderness" areas north of Mexico.

Trading with Europeans

European trade was started by the French in 1534 with Jacques Cartier's voyages along the St. Lawrence River and was expanded in 1603 by Samuel de Champlain. By 1672 the French had set up the Company of New France to compete with the English-owned Hudson's Bay Company. The English company had established its own charter and was granted a trading monopoly in Rupert's Land (Canada) by the British Crown in 1670. It was so firmly associated with trading that ownership of "Bay" blankets became a standard measure of wealth in many northern regions.

European trade and exploration were fueled by a search for new sources of wealth and a desire to obtain power and prestige. Trading routes were improved through better ocean-going ships, more advanced navigation techniques, and more accurate maps. The so-called "New World" offered unbounded opportunities for the satisfaction of European desires, as

LEFT: The knife shown here was made in the 19th century in India—then part of the British Empire. Through trade it found its way into the hands of a Plains warrior, who decorated the sheath with beads.

well as providing ample opportunities for those with a sense of adventure or a thirst for knowledge.

Although France and England were the major trade competitors in North America, other European nations were involved. The Spanish penetrated the continent from the south, via Mexico and Florida, while the Dutch expanded to the northwest along the Hudson River. Russian traders came from Siberia into Alaska and extended their activities south into California.

Wars and alliances

European rivalries in America resulted in dissent and conflict. During the French and Indian War of the mid-18th century France and Britain both relied heavily on alliances with different tribes—alliances originally formed through trading agreements. Similarly, the colonies' decision to break away from England—the American Revolutionary War, leading to the formation of the United States in 1776—was inspired by their refusal to pay tax to a remote English parliament where their interests were not represented.

Following independence, American and Canadian policy continued to favor tribes with whom profitable trade relationships could be maintained. It is true that European—and later American and Canadian—trade contacts were established on the basis of the needs of those nations. However, at the same time these contacts also made the tribes with whom the Europeans dealt dependent on European goods and trade.

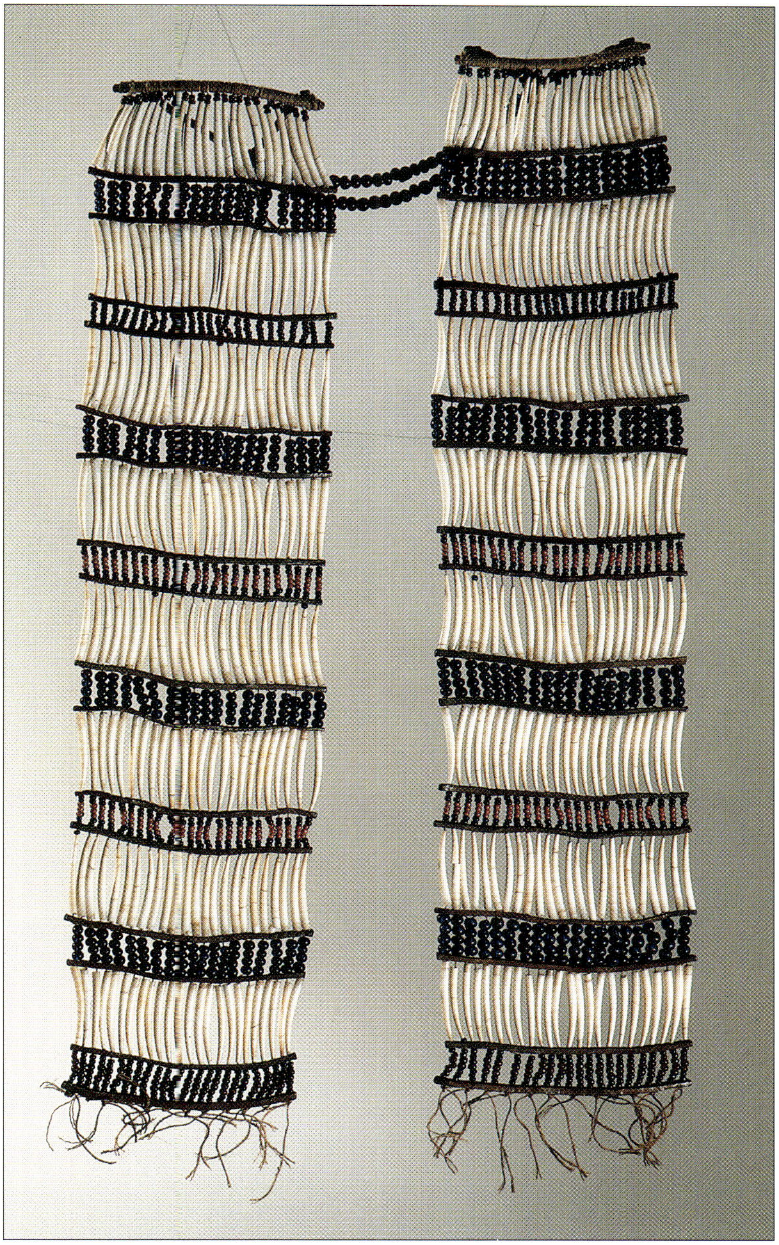

ABOVE: "Tusk" seashells were valued as trade items by the Nootka of the Northwest Coast. Here they are strung with glass beads as a girl's hair ornament.

Reliance on Europeans

Firearms were preeminent among early European trade goods, since tribes armed with them could establish superior.ty over tribes armed only with native weapons. But guns required ammunition, which was obtainable only from Europeans. In this way a cycle was created in which Native-American tribes had no option but to trade with Europeans.

Other European trade goods quickly became a necessary part of everyday native life. They included metal-bladed tools and knives, copper and iron kettles, and trade cloth. However, numerous luxury items were also in regular demand: beads soon came to replace porcupine and bird quills in native decorative embroidery. Native Americans also began to use manufactured dyes and paints in place of traditional natural colors derived from minerals and other sources.

ABOVE: This shaped abalone shell dates from about 1900 and was worn as an ornament by a member of the Kwakiutl tribe of the Northwest Coast. The shell came originally from California—abalone shells in the Northwest were thin and pale, so there was a great trade demand for California shells.

Changing culture

Traded items were so important they completely changed many native cultures. For example, 19th-century Plains culture relied heavily on two items introduced by Europeans—the horse and the gun. They were obtained from trading with Anglo-Americans or acquired through trading with other tribal groups (or raiding them).

But Native-American dependency on European goods was far more widespread than this. The Cree of the Subarctic became dependent on iron traps for hunting, both to secure meat to eat and to get furs to trade. On the Northwest Coast the massive cedar-wood carvings called totem poles developed from smaller carved house-posts only after metal tools replaced earlier bone and shell tools.

For many tribal groups their primary relationship with settlers was through the itinerant (traveling) trader or the trading post. Today the trading post continues to be a symbol of this relationship as well as a major source of income for many Native-American families—either through employment with trading companies or from the sale of artifacts to tourists.

SEE ALSO:
- Adena and Hopewell
- American Revolutionary War
- Basin and Plateau
- Canoes
- Cree
- Firearms
- French and Indian War
- Fur Trade
- Horses
- Hudson's Bay Company
- Northwest Coast
- Plains
- Quillwork and Beadwork
- Tlingit
- Totem Pole
- Woodland

Trail of Tears

The Trail of Tears is the name by which historians remember the removal of great numbers of the Cherokee nation from their ancestral lands. The name refers to the tragedy that struck the Cherokee during the six months' journey between their homeland in North Carolina and their new reservation in what is now Oklahoma. The Cherokee were not the only eastern nation to be taken from their traditional lands, but their removal was the most tragic, for many lives were lost during the 800-mile (1,290 km) trek toward the West.

Indian Removal Act

Like the Cherokee, most Native Americans whose tribes once lived in eastern North America no longer inhabit the lands where European colonizers first came across their ancestors. Powerful nations once inhabited present-day Georgia, Mississippi, Louisiana, and the Carolinas. However, they were forcibly removed by the U.S. government to make room for the increasing numbers of pioneers and settlers who came to the region between the end of the 18th century and the start of the 19th century.

Following the 1830 Indian Removal Act signed by President Andrew Jackson, the tribes living east of the Mississippi River had to be relocated to the new Indian Territory, in the modern-day state of Oklahoma. The Removal Act was not welcomed by the tribes, who had lived on their lands for as long as they could remember.

The native nations involved in the plan put up great resistance to their forced removal, and the

BELOW: The painting shown here by Robert Lindneux depicts the forcible removal of the Cherokee to the Indian Territory in 1838.

Cherokee chief John Ross brought the case to the Supreme Court. Although Ross won his case, President Jackson refused to accept the Supreme Court's decision. The Five Civilized Tribes—the Cherokee, Choctaw, Creek, Seminole, and Chickasaw—were ordered to leave their ancestral homelands.

Suffering of the Tribes

The Choctaw nation was the first to be removed. Settlers from Alabama and Mississippi descended on the tribe as they prepared for their journey, bullying and tricking many out of their moveable goods. The Choctaw were then forced to trek to the Indian Territory during the bitter winter of 1831–1832, the coldest winter since 1776. Nearly one-tenth of the tribe died from the harsh journey and a cholera epidemic. Most of these were children or elderly people.

The Chickasaw from Tennessee were the closest to the Indian Territory and suffered the least during the removal, but cholera hit them too once they arrived there.

The Cherokee put up a fierce resistance to removal from their lands in western Georgia and North Carolina. Some fled to the mountains, where their descendants still live today. Native resistance provided an excuse for the U.S. government to intervene with force against the Cherokee, and the U.S. Army surrounded the Cherokee in preparation for the move.

The removal of the Cherokee began during the spring and summer of 1838 and continued throughout the fall and winter of the same year. The conditions that the Cherokee had to endure were appalling: freezing cold tormented them and made traveling even more difficult, and no adequate food rations were provided. The Cherokee suffered attacks from bandits, and mud and rain made conditions worse. The army forced the tribe to maintain a speed that many found unbearable, and the dead had to be left behind without proper burial.

About 4,000 tribespeople are estimated to have died during the removal. Most lost their lives either in the camps into which they were gathered before the march or during the journey itself. This figure represents one in four of the original number who began the journey.

ABOVE: Chief John Ross, shown here, had a Scottish father and a Cherokee mother. After his successful appeal against the removal of his tribe was overturned by President Jackson, Ross led the Cherokee on the Trail of Tears.

SEE ALSO:
- Disenfranchisement
- Epidemics
- Five Civilized Tribes
- Indian Territory
- Seminole
- Settlers

Travois

Native-American people did not use the wheel. They had no carts, wagons, or any other type of wheeled vehicle, although we know that the concept of the wheel was familiar to them.

Children in Mesoamerica (the area stretching from central Mexico to Nicaragua) often played with wheeled toys, and many wheeled and hooped forms were used in ceremonies throughout North America. One possible reason why Native Americans did not use the wheel may be that they viewed it as a symbol of life and therefore as too sacred an emblem to be used for everyday tasks.

Even in relatively recent periods most Native Americans traveled by foot, and they manufactured a countless variety of packs, baskets, jars, and other containers that could be carried comfortably.

However, the nomadic lifestyle of the Great Plains, where whole tribes moved constantly, gave rise to the travois. It was an A-shaped frame with a closed end that originally fitted over the shoulders of large Native-American dogs that pulled the frame. The free end was left to trail along the ground. A platform on the travois was used to store bundles of belongings, tepee coverings, and other goods.

BELOW: The photograph of these Cree people standing with a horse travois was taken about 1890.

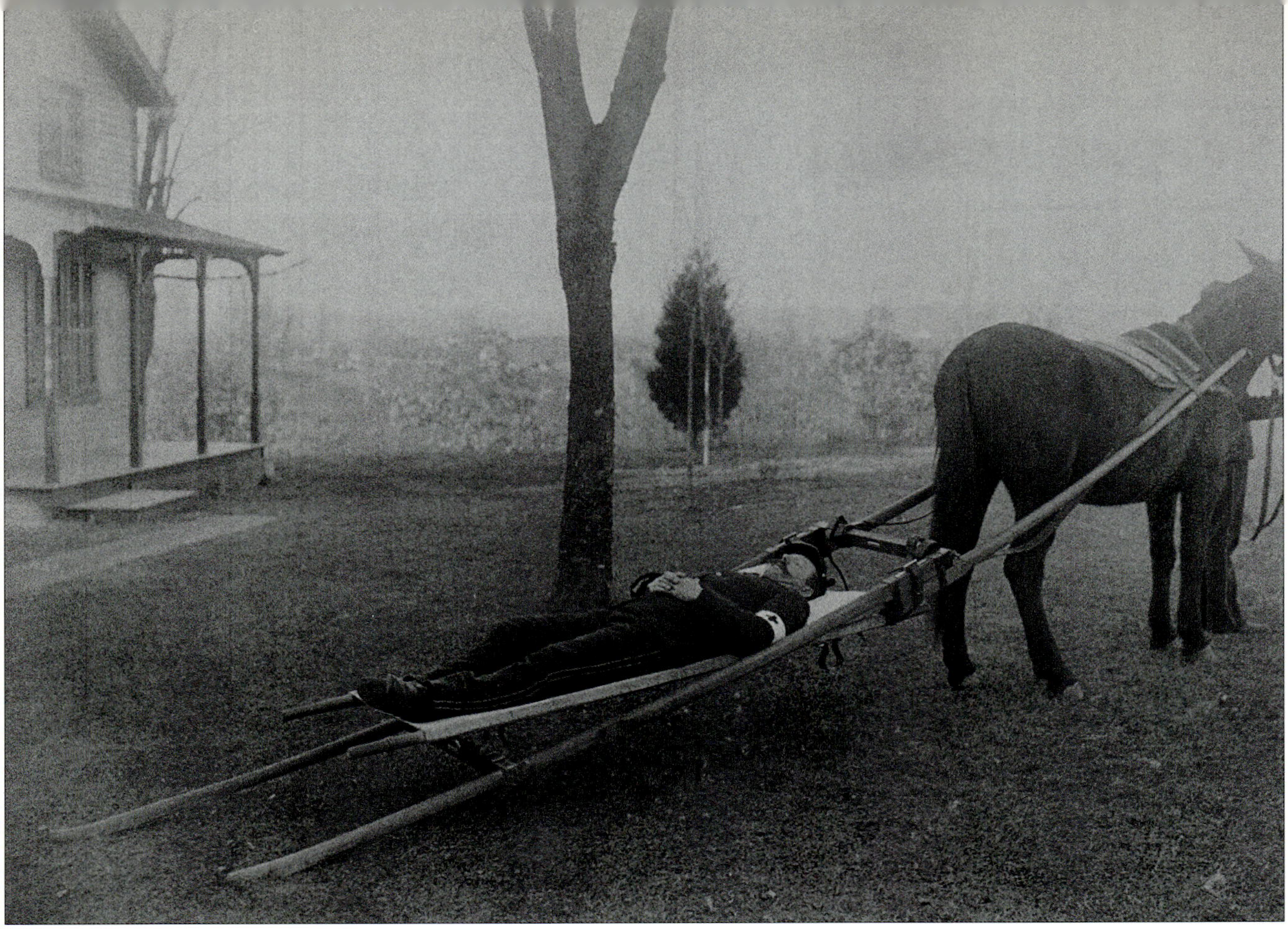

Adaptability of the Travois

In the 16th century the Spanish brought horses to North America, and Plains tribespeople adapted the travois to fit them. The greater size and strength of a horse compared to a dog meant that larger loads could be transported. Use of the horse travois permitted the acquisition of luxury goods and nonessentials that had previously been too difficult to carry.

The horse travois also caused changes in social practice, since it could be used for carrying the elderly, injured, or frail. This development ended the practice of abandoning those who were unable to keep up with the rapid movements of the tribe as it followed migrating game animals.

Large tepees required long poles, and they were often ingeniously used as a makeshift travois frame. Bundles of tepee poles were lashed to either side of a horse, and a spacer bar was used to maintain the A-shape of the frame and to spread the trailing ends of the poles. In this way a Native-American family was able to move greater quantities of goods and larger homes.

Another advantage of the travois was that it could be used on narrow or rutted paths and trails that were impassable to wagons. During the Plains Indian Wars one of the reasons that the tribes could move so rapidly, and therefore evade pursuit, was their ability to use narrow tracks and passes. U.S. troops, who were dependent on bulky supply wagons, found it difficult to follow them.

The travois was so adaptable for use in rugged country that it was adopted as a means of transportation by many French Canadians. It was also widely used during the early days of the logging industry.

ABOVE: The travois had many uses. In this 19th-century photograph a horse travois is being used to move a wounded U.S. soldier.

SEE ALSO:
- Homes
- Horses
- Hunting
- Indian Wars
- Medicine Wheel
- Plains
- Spain, Wars with

Treaties

BELOW: Unlike many of his contemporaries, William Penn treated the Native Americans he met fairly and honored the treaties that he made with them. This painting from the early 19th century shows Penn visiting a tribe in 1682.

Treaties are legal agreements made between opposing sides to settle disputes and define the rights and obligations that each has to the other. Under the terms of the treaties signed between Native Americans and first Europeans and later Americans, white settlers were usually given access to tribal lands. In return Native Americans received guarantees that their own properties and interests would be protected and that their rights to self-government would be recognized.

Historically, treaties were signed as arrangements made between sovereign (or independent) nations. This means that Native-American tribes were considered as independent governments. So tribes that signed treaties with the U.S. in the 19th century, for example, can today make and enforce their own laws, set their own taxes, determine tribal membership and access to reservation areas, and control the ways in which their lands are used.

Early treaties

The first treaties signed by Native Americans were made with European powers seeking lands on which to establish their colonies and farms. At this time individual Native Americans did not own land. However, the treaties were necessary so that different European nations could legally claim particular areas and defend them against other European nations.

Native Americans did receive benefits from the treaties in the form of European trade goods to compensate for the loss of land. Native peoples were also recognized by Europeans as "legal owners" who were officially entitled to sell the lands they occupied.

LEFT: This late 19th-century photograph shows a Crow delegation that visited Washington to negotiate a treaty.

New arrangements

When the colonies declared their independence, many old treaties were renegotiated. The first of these was made with the Delaware tribe in 1778, but most treaties were signed during the mid-19th century.

Under these new agreements treaties had to be ratified (or agreed) by Congress. Although native tribes were still considered to be sovereign nations, the power they had to govern themselves was limited by the U.S. government. The system in Canada was only slightly different in that Canadian treaties were held in trust by the Canadian government on behalf of the British Crown.

Injustice and removal

Many renegotiated treaties were forced on the tribes. Some tribes were decimated by wars and new diseases brought by settlers. They had little choice but to accept treaties that gave them provisions or face starvation and extinction. Other treaties were fraudulent or deceptive. Their terms were explained by interpreters employed by the U.S. government. These people often misled tribes into believing they were guaranteed certain rights that were not mentioned in the treaties.

For many nations treaties meant removal from their homelands. The Cherokee, for example, signed the New Echota Treaty in 1835, which resulted in them being moved to the Indian Territory (present-day Oklahoma) and losing their original lands. Most of the tribe disagreed with the treaty, but a few individuals who were bribed by the government to pose as "chiefs" signed the agreement that led to the removal of the entire tribe.

The Cherokee had to be marched to their new lands in chains under an army guard because so many refused to go, and many died on the way. Their removal is known today as the Cherokee Trail of Tears. Other tribes in the Southeast—the Creek, Chickasaw, and Choctaw—all suffered a similar fate. Those who stood up for their rights were classed as "hostiles" and were mercilessly hunted down by the U.S. Army.

There are many other cases in which renegotiated treaties were not beneficial to the tribes involved. Nevertheless, the government in Washington considered the treaties valid, and the tribes were refused permission to appeal against them. Under federal law these new treaties and the conditions they imposed replaced any previous treaties the tribes had signed.

Resentment and conflict

Most of the U.S. treaties served the interests of the white communities and were intended to protect settlers and pioneers moving through or into Native-American lands. Native Americans often resented these incursions because wagon trains—and later railroads—disturbed the migration routes of animals the tribes relied on, such as buffalo, and frightened other animals away. Some tribes, particularly those of the Great Plains, resisted treaties and fought wars to keep their lands safe, but the superior military power of the U.S. eventually defeated them.

Fighting often broke out when the tribes realized they had been misled, when Congress failed to agree on new treaties, or when white settlers and hunters invaded tribal lands in violation of treaty agreements. In most cases the U.S. government failed in its obligations to protect Native-American property.

BELOW: The treaty shown here was signed at the end of Pontiac's War in 1796. It features both the signatures of officers representing the British forces and symbols that stand for the leaders of the Native-American tribes.

The nature of the treaties and the aggressive attitude adopted toward native rights at the time are illustrated by the fact that the Bureau of Indian Affairs—then responsible for looking after Native-American interests—was part of the Department of War. It was not until 1849 that the bureau moved to the Department of the Interior and was no longer under military control.

Cultural misunderstandings

By the end of the 1850s the United States had signed 370 treaties with different tribes. Many of the treaties indicate that Native-American

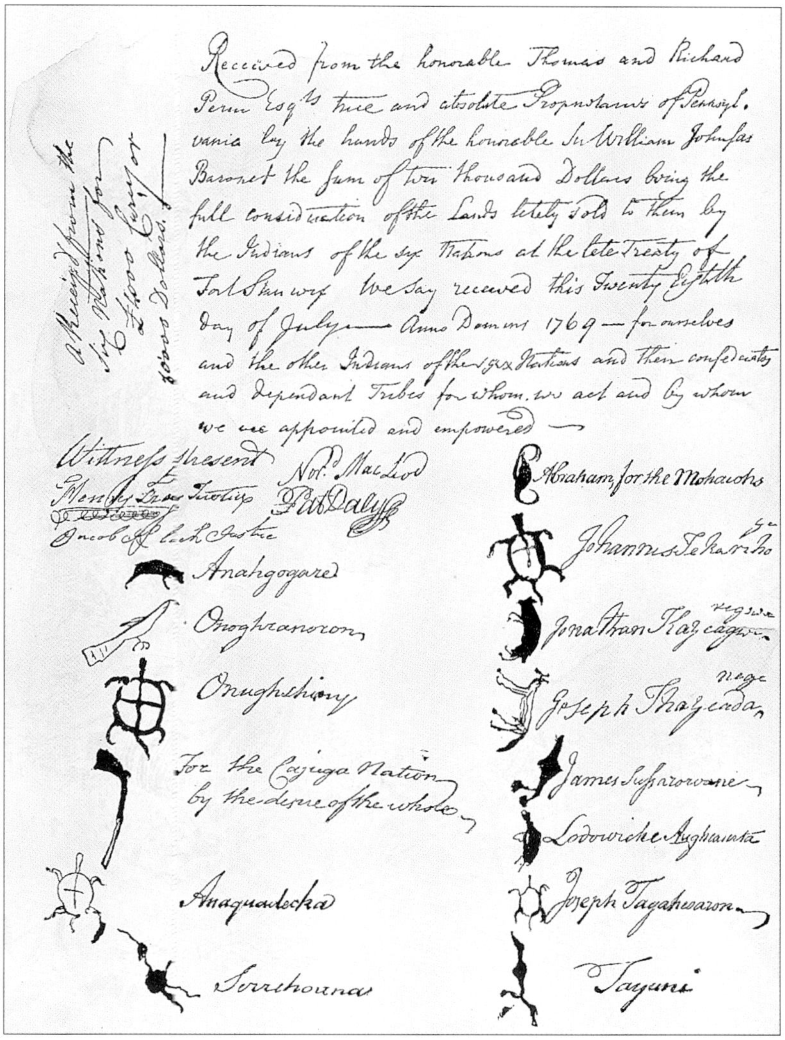

Received from the honorable Thomas and Richard Penn Esq[rs] true and absolute Proprietaries of Pennsylvania by the hands of the honorable Sir William Johnson Baronet the Sum of Ten thousand Dollars being the full consideration of the Lands lately sold to them by the Indians of the Six Nations at the late Treaty of Fort Stanwix We say received this Twenty Eighth day of July — Anno Domini 1769 — for ourselves and the other Indians of the Six Nations and their confederates and dependant Tribes for whom we act and by whom we are appointed and empowered —

Witness present Nor[d] MacLeod Pat Daly

Anahgogare
Onoghranoron
Onughshiony
For the Cayuga Nation by the desire of the whole
Anaquadecka
Serrihouna

Abraham for the Mohawks
Johannes Tekarihoga
Jonathan Kayenagweregswa
Joseph Thayendanega
James Sussarowane
Lodowicke Aughsanta
Joseph Tagahesaron
Tayuni

ABOVE: This photograph from 1868 shows the signing of the Fort Laramie Treaty.

attitudes and cultures had been misunderstood and that respect for the land—which was so vital to native people—was of little concern when that land was required for settlement. Treaty provisions were often unworkable, and agreements were regularly broken. By 1870 it was becoming clear that the treaties were unrealistic, and an official end to treaty-making was declared by an act of Congress in 1871.

Protest and Broken Promises

More recently, the subject of treaties has been raised once more. In 1972 the issue of unkept treaty promises was brought up by the American Indian Movement activists. They organized a march on Washington called the "Trail of Broken Treaties Caravan" and occupied the offices of the Bureau of Indian Affairs. The intention was to raise public awareness and highlight the unresolved issues arising from broken treaty agreements.

In 1977 the American Indian Policy Review Commission was set up. It published a paper specifying that native peoples have the right to self-determination and self-government, thus insuring them sovereignty on their lands. Nevertheless, funding to enable Native Americans to become self-sufficient has been restricted since the 1980s.

Today Native Americans argue against the loss of rights to which they believe they are legally entitled by claiming that this is a violation of the U.S. Constitution. Instead of armed conflicts a refusal to recognize treaty agreements is now argued out within the confines of the courtroom.

SEE ALSO:
- Bureau of Indian Affairs
- Delaware
- Disenfranchisement
- Indian Territory
- Interpreters
- Land Rights
- Pan-Indian Movement
- Plains
- Railroads
- Reservations
- Trail of Tears

Tsimshian

BELOW: Wearing traditional dress, the son of a Tsimshian totem-pole carver dances and bangs a drum at a totem-pole-raising ceremony.

The Tsimshian live in 14 separate villages beside the Skeena and Nass rivers on the Pacific Coast of Alaska and British Columbia and on nearby islands. Each village name includes the word "Git" or "Kit" (meaning "people of"), followed by a name referring to the part of the river the village is next to.

The Tsimshian are closely related to other Northwest Coast groups, such as the Gitksan, whose legends say they come from a town in the interior of the United States called Temlaxam, or Prairie Town. The Tsimshian language may, however, be distantly related to Penutian, which is spoken by tribes living farther south, in the states of Washington, Oregon, and California.

The Tsimshian maintain a traditional way of life. Many of them work seasonally in the logging and fishing industries, but they still consider winter to be a sacred ceremonial season. There is also a strong revival of traditional crafts at villages such as Ksan, which has become a heritage craft and cultural center for the tribe.

Although the Tsimshian live mostly on products from the sea and rivers, they also hunt in the inland forests for deer, bear, and

ABOVE: Tsimshian people wear highly colorful clothing and play ornately decorated drums at totem-pole-raising ceremonies.

mountain goats and forage for wild foods such as berries and roots. Fish is the Tsimshian's most important food, and the region has a plentiful supply. In spring they fish for salmon and eulachon (candlefish), which swim up the rivers from the sea in great numbers. During the rest of the year they catch fish such as halibut, cod, and flounder from the sea.

In the past the Tsimshian also hunted sea mammals such as seals and sea otters, which provided materials for tools, clothes, and blankets, as well as food.

The Tsimshian used to fish from dugout canoes, which they also used for transport, trading with neighboring tribes along the coast. One of their most important trade goods was eulachon oil, which came only from the Tsimshian area but was highly prized by other tribes on the coast. They obtained blankets woven from dog and goat hair from the Chilkat (a Tlingit tribe), which were richly decorated with animals and figures relating to clan totems. The skill of Tsimshian woodcarvers was such that there was wide trade demand for their masks and other items.

Under one roof

Tsimshian homes are large, one-story houses made from wooden planks. Each has one main room with sleeping platforms built around the walls and a fireplace in the center. Partitioned off from this main living area is a smaller room at the back of the house. Here ceremonial items such as masks are kept when they are not being used.

As many as 30 or 40 people live in each house. The people in each house are all members of the same household clan—people who claim descent from a common legendary ancestor—together with other family members who have married into the clan. Tsimshian clans are matrilineal, meaning that people's kinships are determined through descent from their mothers.

A class-based society

Tsimshian society, like that of other Northwest Coast tribes, is divided into classes. The highest class comprises heads of households, or chiefs. Below them are nobles, and beneath the nobles are common people. Before they were influenced by European ideals, the Tsimshian valued personal wealth highly, and many rich families adopted captives from other tribes. These captives were thought of as the "property" of their owners. They are sometimes referred to as "slaves" because they had few rights or privileges, but their lives were generally no more harsh than those of common Tsimshian people.

The spiritual life of the Tsimshian is complex. Like the Haida and Tlingit, they have powerful shamans (medicine men and women) who preside over the activities of secret societies. The most important of these are the Mitla (Those Who Descend from the Heavens) and Nutlem (Wolf Society).

In the past when people were seriously ill, Tsimshian shamans tried to cure them by using hollow ivory tubes called "soul-catchers" in special rituals. This was because the Tsimshian traditionally believed that illness was caused by the soul, or spirit, leaving the body. They still use soul-catchers when someone is ill—performing such traditional rituals helps maintain tribal identity—but always in conjunction with modern medicine.

BELOW: Worn by a Tsimshian shaman, this ceremonial headdress is in the form of a squirrel.

Tsimshian potlatches

Another tradition the Tsimshian retain is the holding of potlatches, or "giveaways." These are celebrations at which a family holds a feast and claims ownership of masks, crests, and other privileges by giving out goods to its guests. By accepting the gifts, the guests recognize the claims of their hosts.

Fact File

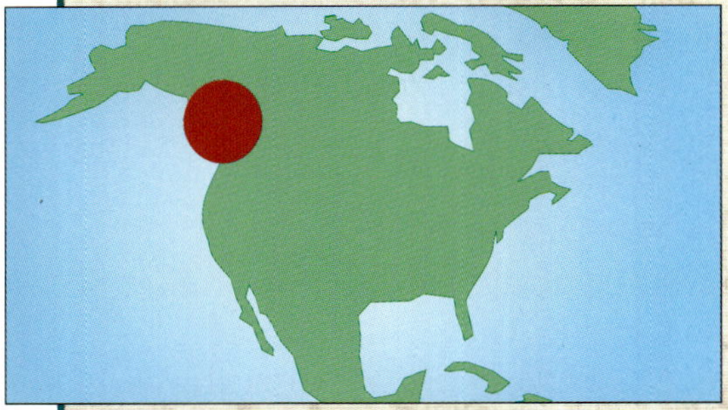

The Tsimshian live beside two main rivers on the Northwest Coast.

LANGUAGE:	*Tsimshian*
AREA:	*Coastal rivers and islands in British Columbia and Alaska*
RESERVATION:	*Village and island reservations in their traditional homeland*
POPULATION:	*About 2,400 today*
HOUSING:	*One-story wooden houses*
EUROPEAN CONTACT:	*Explorers, missionaries, and traders in the 18th and 19th centuries*
NEIGHBORS:	*Tlingit and Haida*
LIFESTYLE:	*Based on fishing; live in settled villages*
FOOD:	*Fish, especially salmon; some game and wild foods such as berries*
CRAFTS:	*Memorial totem poles, copper ornaments and tools, woodwork, and basketry*

European contact

From the mid-1700s the main European powers, especially Russia and England, sent expeditions along the Northwest Coast but did not try to settle there. They did trade with the Tsimshian, however, and by the 1780s the exchange of sea-otter furs for metal goods had made the northern Northwest Coast a center of commerce. By the 1830s the Hudson's Bay Company had trading posts in the area at Fort Simpson and Fort Essington—although the fur trade had declined by then.

In the 1860s William Duncan, a Scottish preacher, arrived with the aim of converting the Tsimshian to Christianity. Duncan studied their language and mythology and in 1862 succeeded in converting several chiefs. He built a mission at Metlakatla, intending that the Tsimshian should give up their own culture and live in model villages of European-style houses, where they could learn skills such as carpentry and blacksmithing. He also set up a fish-canning factory and a sawmill.

In 1887 the British government decided to place the Tsimshian living in British Columbia on reservations. The Tsimshian appealed to Queen Victoria in vain and hired lawyers to protect their land rights. The court cases went on until 1927, when the Tsimshian were forbidden to pursue the matter any further.

SEE ALSO:
- Canoes
- Clan
- Fishing
- Fur Trade
- Haida
- Homes
- Hudson's Bay Company
- Land Rights
- Missions
- Northwest Coast
- Potlatch
- Reservations
- Salmon
- Shamanism
- Tlingit
- Totemism
- Totem Pole
- Trade

Tula

RIGHT: The Pyramid of the Morning Star at Tula. The 10th-century columns seen in the photograph would have supported a giant roof long since vanished.

Tula is situated about 250 miles (400 km) north of Mexico City in the state of Hidalgo. It is thought the city was founded by the Toltec, who called it Tollan and made it their capital. Between the 11th and 12th centuries, however, internal problems led to Tollan losing its power. Today Tula is a town with a population of 42,000.

Topiltzin (also called Quetzalcoatl), the first Toltec leader, is believed to have founded the city and led the empire through its first great period of building, arts, and trade. Toltec influence spread as far as present-day Costa Rica and the southwestern United States.

Tula covered 5 square miles (13 sq. km), and its population grew to number some 60,000. The elite of the city prospered from the control of trade in obsidian (a dark volcanic rock), which was used to make weapons and household utensils. It is thought a warrior faction came to dominate the capital in the late 10th century. It extended the empire until, in the 12th century, civil conflict, war with a fierce nomadic group (probably the Chichimec ancestors of the Aztecs), and a great fire led to the decline of the city. During this time almost half the population of Tula moved to Capultepec on the bank of Lake Texcoco (now part of Mexico City).

Architecture of Tula

The five-tiered Pyramid of the Morning Star dominated the ceremonial center of Tula. It featured four stone statues of warriors, each 15 feet (4.5 m) high, which originally helped support the roof of the sanctuary. The statues (called *atlantes*) wore plumed headdresses and breastplates and carried spear-throwers (called *atlatls*) and javelins. Meant to represent Quetzalcoatl, these figures were originally painted red, blue, black, and white. It is possible that the pyramid derives its name from the legend that Quetzalcoatl rose into the sky like a burning bird to become the Morning Star.

The Burned Palace has two giant chacmools, which are reclining statues that were probably used to hold sacrifices. The center of the city contained ball courts, pyramids, and palaces decorated with carved panels, which were originally painted. Many of the carvings depict gods, eagles, and jaguars. Carvings of warriors are also common, reflecting the warlike character of the Toltec.

SEE ALSO:
- Aztecs
- Chitchén Itzá
- Copán
- Maya
- Palenque
- Pyramids
- Tenochtitlán
- Toltec

Upper Missouri Tribes

To the east of the Great Plains the Missouri River marks one of the traditional boundaries of the Upper Missouri region, snaking eastward and south from the Rocky Mountains. Originally, Plains tribes were farmers and lived in semipermanent dwellings. These tribes had moved into the area from the Eastern Woodland area. They lived in settlements of earth-covered lodges along the Upper Missouri River and its tributaries in modern-day North Dakota.

The introduction of horses by the Spanish in the 16th century created a new, nomadic way of life for most tribespeople. Those tribes that remained in semipermanent settlements formed a subgroup of the Plains culture as a whole—the Upper Missouri tribal region. This group divides into two language groups: the Siouan-speaking Mandan and Hidatsa, and the Caddoan-speaking Arikara.

THE MANDAN LIFESTYLE

Probably the most influential Upper Missouri tribe was the Mandan. The people were farmers and hunters. They grew corn, beans, squash, and sunflowers and hunted buffalo and elk. During the spring and summer they fished.

The Mandan lived in villages of semiunderground earth lodges. Each village was surrounded by a palisade (a fence of stakes) for defense.

When a French fur-trade expedition encountered the Mandan in 1738, the tribe was living in nine villages situated hundreds of miles apart along the bank of the Missouri River. Each settlement was made up of several dozen households arranged on terraced land. The villages were independent social and economic units, with the tribe being, in effect, the villages combined.

A smallpox epidemic in 1781 reduced the Mandan population severely; and when Lewis and Clark

BELOW: Karl Bodmer produced this 19th-century lithograph of an Arikara man.

visited the Mandan in 1804, only two villages were left. In the 1830s the artists George Catlin and Karl Bodmer visited these villages and recorded their impressions of Mandan culture in a series of famous paintings.

Mandan earth lodges were about 50 feet (15 m) long and 30 feet (9 m) wide, with a central pole and two large entrance posts. Early lodges were rectangular, though the Mandan started building circular lodges about 1500. The floor was dug into the earth, and the wooden slats of the roof were covered with earth and grass.

A trading people

A second smallpox epidemic in 1837 almost destroyed the Mandan. Even so, the villages remained a commercial and trading focal point for areas to the north, west, and east. These trade links enabled the tribe to obtain metal tools from the Cree to the north and to forge relations with the nomadic Mountain Crow to the west. In turn, the Mountain Crow gave the Mandan access to the horse-trading Plateau tribes.

In the villages of the Upper Missouri mules, bridles, and blankets were traded with tribes from the Southwest. Guns, kettles, and axes were traded from the English and French in the north. The Missouri was the focal point of a complex and intertribal trading network in which the Mandan, Hidatsa, and Arikara were middlemen. The acquisition of guns and horses in particular marked the birth of "traditional" Plains culture, the heyday of which lasted from about 1800 to 1870.

ABOVE: The portrait of Chief Shahaka of the Mandan tribe shown here was painted by Charles Bird King.

Other Upper Missouri tribes

The Hidatsa were a seminomadic people strongly associated with the River Crow; both tribes spoke Siouan languages. The Hidatsa learned to grow corn from the Mandan and farmed the Upper Missouri region of North Dakota at its meeting point with the Heart and Knife rivers. The Hidatsa lived in villages of round, domed earth lodges. They were also the best-known tobacco growers and were deeply involved in the gun and horse trades.

Farther south the Arikara were the trading link to the Cheyenne and Teton Sioux. Their Caddoan language ties them to the Pawnee, but they have been separate groups for at least 500 years. Early French fur traders identified the Arikara settlement at the Grand River as a good place to access the Plains trade network and obtain furs and pelts. However, smallpox and conflict with the Sioux eventually took a heavy toll on the Arikara.

Rituals and beliefs

The religious practices of the Missouri tribes were similar to those of Plains culture in general. Although each tribe had its own particular ceremonies, all the Missouri tribes had rich buffalo mythologies.

The tribes believed deeply in the mystery and power of nature. They derived great strength from supernatural visions and from celebrating and praising the natural world in rituals such as the Mandan Okipa ritual. This ceremony dramatized the creation of the Earth, its people, animals, and plants, and symbolically renewed the world for another year. The Okipa was performed every summer. The Mandan believed that by performing the ceremony regularly, they would guarantee plentiful buffalo herds and good fortune for the coming year.

Tribal society

There was a genuine democracy among the Upper Missouri tribes in that tribespeople were entitled to freedom of thought and action. Respect was gained through exemplary deeds rather than by hereditary right. Tribal leaders emerged by force of personality, wisdom, and persuasiveness.

Male and female societies played an important role in the everyday life of the Missouri tribes. Among the Mandan, for example, the Buffalo Society that Karl Bodmer

LEFT: This map shows the spread of the Upper Missouri tribes—the Hidatsa, Mandan, and Arikara—and the location of the neighboring Native-American tribes.

ABOVE: George Catlin painted this depiction of the Mandan Bull Dance about 1833.

painted was the best known and most prestigious. Usually, these societies were age-graded, since the Missouri tribes tended to organize social groupings for both sexes by age. People progressed through societies during their life, gradually assuming certain responsibilities and influence within their tribe.

The roles of women's societies varied. Younger women often concentrated on the building of skills in skinwork and quillwork, while older women were involved with agricultural duties and rites. The most prestigious society for Hidatsa women was the White Buffalo Society. Its members danced in ceremonies to lure buffalo for the men of the tribe to hunt. In the winter the Buffalo Calling ceremony was held to bring buffalo close to the village so that the men would not have far to go to hunt.

THE THREE AFFILIATED TRIBES

After the smallpox epidemic of 1837 devastated both the Hidatsa and Mandan, the survivors of both tribes joined together at Fort Berthold reservation, North Dakota, in 1845. They were joined there in 1862 by the Arikara, whose population had been halved by smallpox, and formed the Three Affiliated Tribes.

By then the developments that took place during the growth of the fur trade had eroded the Missouri tribes' preeminence as trading centers. European contact had been devastating for the tribes both in terms of disease and commerce.

SEE ALSO:
- Buffalo
- Crow
- Epidemics
- Fur Trade
- Hunters
- Plains
- Reservations
- Ritual
- Siouan Speakers
- Southwest
- Trade

Urban Life

Since the end of the World War II in 1945 there has been a massive increase in the number of Native Americans who choose to live in cities rather than on reservations.

Before 1940 about 10 percent of Native Americans lived in cities. However, during World War II many native people joined the armed services or worked in jobs away from their reservations. In this way they broke a number of traditional ties with reservation life.

Migration to the cities

During the 1950s and 1960s the U.S. government encouraged native people to relocate in cities. As a result, many people moved away from the reservations. According to U.S. census counts, 13 percent of the Native-American population lived in urban communities in 1950. In 1960 this figure had increased to 28 percent, but by 1970 it had risen to 45 percent—a level at which it has remained.

The largest urban population of Native Americans is in Oakland, just outside San Francisco, but there are also large communities in major cities such as Tulsa, Oklahoma City, New York, Chicago, and Phoenix.

The move to cities arose because of extreme poverty and low living standards on the reservations. Cities offered better jobs, higher income, and improved education, as well as government-subsidized housing and services. However, Native Americans who moved to cities found prejudice and discrimination. The pace of city life was very different from that on the reservations, and many Native Americans could not cope economically with competition from whites or from large and well-established minority groups.

LEFT: In 1980 a group of Native Americans marched from San Francisco to the United Nations building in New York, protesting against the rights and living conditions of Native Americans in both rural and urban areas. The group is seen here crossing New York's George Washington Bridge.

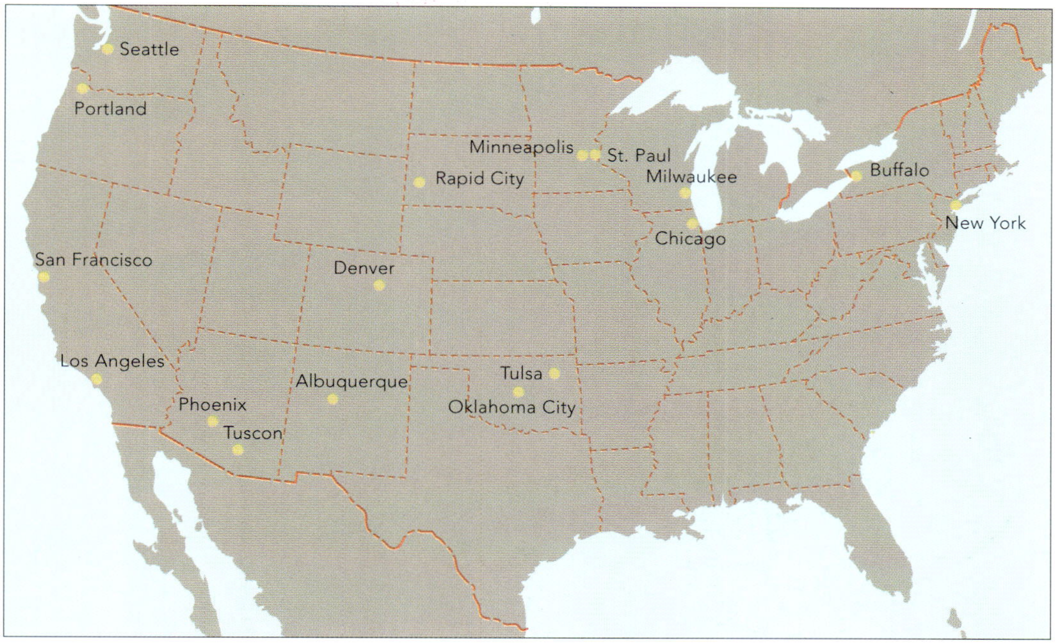

LEFT: This map shows the 17 cities with the highest Native-American population in the U.S.

Native identity

Native Americans also experienced difficulty in finding an identity as a group that shared common goals and common problems. Los Angeles, for example, contains about 30 Native-American groups, each of which exists independently from the others.

For many Native Americans urban life is a depressing experience. Many native people live in run-down areas with few amenities, where they feel isolated from the local community as well as from the traditional values of the reservations.

Combating the problem

Since the 1960s and 1970s efforts have been made to tackle the problems facing urban Native Americans. Some help has come from federally funded programs, such as those of the Department of Health, Education, and Welfare. Other projects have been sponsored by local church groups. However, the most significant effort has come from Native Americans themselves.

Some well-established Native-American organizations, such as the National Council of American Indians, target urban problems and maintain counselling centers. Newer, often more aggressive and radical groups have also formed to tackle these issues. San Francisco has a group called United Native Americans, Minneapolis has the American Indian Movement, and American Indians United is based in Chicago. There are many other similar groups in cities throughout the U.S.

All the groups seek to unite Native Americans and build a sense of history and identity. Through their activities Native-American issues have been brought to public attention. Today native people are developing a pride in their culture and realizing they are a powerful force, not a powerless minority.

SEE ALSO:
- Education
- Pan-Indian Movement
- Population Density
- Poverty
- Reservations

Uto-Aztecan

The Uto-Aztecan language is named after its most prominent northern and southern speakers—the Ute, from the Great Basin in Idaho and Utah, and the Aztecs, from Mexico. It was spoken by numerous other tribes in California, the Great Basin, the Southwest, and south to Tabasco in Mexico.

The most important of these, besides the Ute and Aztecs, were the Paiute and Shoshoni in the north; the Hopi Pueblo and their neighbors the Papago and Pima in the Southwest; the Comanche of the southern Plains; the Mono and Mission tribes, such as the Luiseño and Cahuilla, in California; and several tribes in Mexico, including the Yaqui and Tarahumara.

Similar but different

These and other tribes who spoke Uto-Aztecan were the most diverse and widespread language group in the Western states. They shared a language but had little else in common. The Ute and the Aztecs, for example, lived far apart, in very different environments, and had very different cultures, customs, and lifestyles. Living in extremely hostile and barren terrain, the Ute were hunter-gatherers. Unable to grow crops or rear animals, they lived on whatever berries, roots, and small game they could find. The Aztecs, by contrast, controlled an empire that was based on city-states and advanced agriculture and trade.

The variety in the lifestyles and cultures of the different tribes that spoke Uto-Aztecan is reflected in the fact that some scholars include the Tanoan languages as part of a larger language family called Aztec-Tanoan. The Tanoan languages were spoken by Pueblo groups of the Southwest (the Tiwa, Towa, and Tewa) and by the Kiowa, who were a nomadic Plains tribe. The connections between Uto-Aztecan and Tanoan are unclear, though.

Uto-Aztecan is still spoken today in many areas. Education programs have recently been established to insure that future generations understand the speech of their ancestors and that Uto-Aztecan continues as a living language.

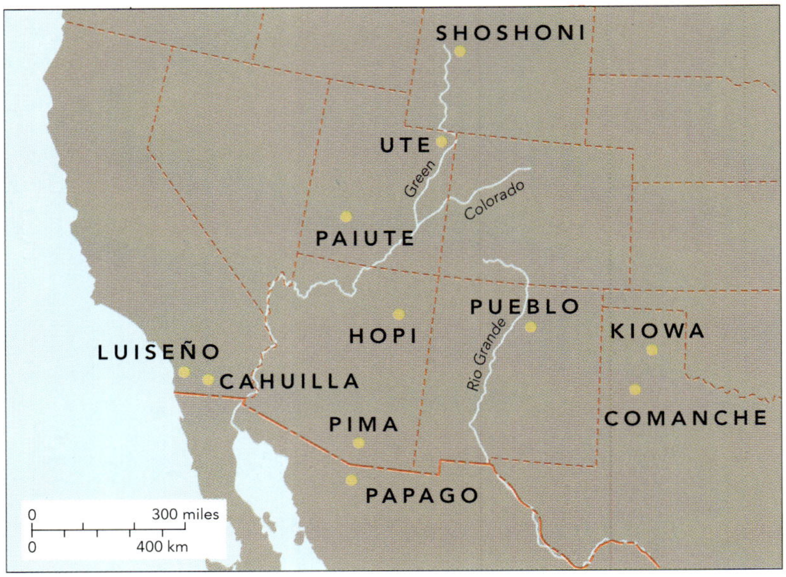

ABOVE: This map shows the original wide-ranging locations of the main tribes in the Uto-Aztecan language group.

SEE ALSO:

- Aztecs
- Basin and Plateau
- Californian Tribal Groups
- Comanche
- Hopi
- Kiowa
- Mission Indians
- Missions
- Paiute
- Papago and Pima
- Plains
- Pueblo
- Southwest
- Tanoan Speakers

Uxmal

The ruins of the Mayan city of Uxmal lie in the Puuc hills in the Yucatán Peninsula of southeastern Mexico. The city remains one of the finest Mayan sites yet to be discovered.

Despite a series of archaeological investigations that began with Jean Frederic de Waldeck in 1836, it is still not clearly understood who built Uxmal. However, it is most likely that the city's foundation was laid in the 6th century by the Maya from present-day Guatemala.

"Uxmal" is the Mayan word for "thrice built." During the height of its power, about A.D. 600–900, the city dominated a series of outlying areas covering 64 square miles (166 sq. km). Uxmal was then abandoned, but from the 11th century onward it was occupied by the Mayan Xiu clan. The Xiu made the city a center of the League of Mayapán, uniting it with the cities of Chitchén Itzá and Mayapán. Uxmal declined, however, after rebellions destroyed the league about 1194. The Spanish later uncovered the city in the 16th century.

Architecture of the City

Uxmal was built in the distinctive Puuc style. Thin squares of limestone veneer were used as facings for buildings, and columns were repeated in long rows. The upper facades of buildings of Uxmal featured impressive stone mosaics of monster masks and latticelike geometric designs.

One of the most imposing structures in Uxmal is the three-tiered Pyramid of the Magician, which rises 125 feet (38 m) at a steep angle. It was built in five stages, with two earlier structures being buried by later additions.

Another impressive building in Uxmal is the Governor's Palace, which has an elaborate frontage of carvings and mosaics dominated by a carving of Uxmal's greatest ruler, Lord Chac—named after a rain god—who probably lived in the palace. Built on a pyramid, the palace is 330 feet (100 m) long and 26 feet (8 m) high. It remains one of the finest buildings in Mesoamerica (the area stretching from central Mexico to Nicaragua).

The rain god Chac was very important to the people of Uxmal. The city depended on rainwater, which was carefully collected. It is possible that Uxmal's inhabitants had to abandon the city on several occasions during severe droughts.

ABOVE: The Governor's Palace at Uxmal is richly decorated with carvings and mosaics and is one of the best-preserved ancient buildings in Mesoamerica.

SEE ALSO:
- Chitchén Itzá
- Maya
- Mitla
- Palenque
- Tikal

Vision Quest

A Vision Quest is an attempt by an individual to gain the help of a supernatural being to solve a particular problem or to provide general guidance over a lifetime. Vision Quests are more common among Native Americans who originally lived east of the Rockies than among those who lived west of the mountain range. They are particularly associated with the peoples of the Plains, such as the Shoshoni, Cheyenne, and Lakota Sioux.

A TEST OF MIND AND BODY

A Vision Quest is an intensely sacred activity. It is not undertaken lightly because it involves a great deal of physical and psychological stress. Although some people are thought capable of receiving a vision more easily than others, most people seeking a vision need the advice and help of a shaman (a medicine man or woman). Under the guidance of the shaman the vision-seeker does a great deal of ritual preparation.

The first stage is for the vision-seeker to gather various items that the shaman requires. They may include different scented grasses and herbs, particular stones or other minerals, and sometimes the feathers or skin of specific birds or animals. Tobacco is also necessary for the vision-seeker and the shaman to smoke as a prayer offering to the spirits with whom contact is sought. All these items have to be ritually prepared and blessed before they can be used.

The next step is for the vision-seeker to undergo a purification ritual. Native Americans believe that to attempt to approach the spirit world in an unpurified state is highly dangerous. Purification can involve taking a sweat bath, drinking an herbal concoction that causes vomiting, or undergoing smudging—burning a sacred material, such as cedar wood, sage, or sweetgrass, and blowing the smoke over the body.

During and after purification the vision-seeker prays constantly. These prayers are requests for the strength to withstand the power of the supernatural world should it come in a vision.

Finally, the vision-seeker goes into the wilderness to fast (go without food or drink) and chant and possibly go without sleep.

ABOVE: This 19th-century photograph is of a Sioux shaman called White Bull. Before going on a Vision Quest, most Native Americans need to seek the help and advice of a shaman.

The vision-seeker looks for a place far away from other people, such as the top of a high mesa, or a dangerous place, such as a path frequently used by bears. In this way the vision-seeker demonstrates the sacrifices he or she is prepared to make and the dangers he or she is willing to overcome in order to show faith in the protective power of the spirits.

The vision, when it comes, gives a clear indication to the seeker about what to do next. Often the spirit appears in the form of a bird or animal, which instructs the seeker on how best to live and what precautions to take when next approaching the spirit world. Often, it also gives him or her a song and ways to paint the face and body when next trying to contact the spirit.

RIGHT: This 1950s picture depicts "Custer's Last Stand" at Little Bighorn in 1876. The Sioux leader and shaman Sitting Bull famously foresaw Custer's defeat in a vision he received on a Vision Quest.

SEE ALSO:

- Body Adornment
- Cheyenne
- Fasting
- Little Bighorn
- Medicine
- Peyote
- Plains
- Ritual
- Shamanism
- Sioux
- Sitting Bull
- Sun Dance
- Sweat Lodge
- Tobacco

Wagon Trails

The United States grew rapidly after the American Revolutionary War. In 1783 it owned lands that extended only to the Mississippi and Missouri rivers, but by the middle of the 19th century it had spread across the continent to the West Coast. At the heart of this expansion were pioneer prospectors and settlers, urged on by promises of a better, more prosperous future and encouraged by government-subsidized land grants.

The only way westward, before a transcontinental railroad link was completed in 1869, was by horse-drawn covered wagons, which had to be large enough to carry everything the pioneers owned. The pioneers followed old Native-American trails, many of which had been enlarged and improved as military roads. Even so, travel was difficult. The terrain was often rough, slowing the progress of the heavily laden wagons. There was also a constant threat from Native Americans who resented the intrusion of settlers and wagon trains, since they frightened away many of the animals the tribespeople hunted and depended on for their survival.

West to the promised land

For the pioneers, however, the West was a promised land—a country of fertile valleys in which to settle and farm or of great wealth to be obtained from gold prospecting. The wagon trails led to opportunities that could never be realized in the East. Unfortunately, the trails also crossed tribal lands that had been reserved exclusively for Native-American use. In 1763 the British government, which ruled the territory at that time, had drawn up the Proclamation Line, which was

BELOW: This 19th-century engraving of General Miles's military expedition against the Sioux depicts a column of U.S. Army wagons moving along a trail through Montana.

ABOVE: One of the best-known wagon routes was the Oregon Trail, parts of which are still used as dirt roads.

devised to keep colonists and Native Americans apart. But this meant little to the pioneers, who did not care that they were trespassing on Native-American lands in violation of treaty agreements.

THE RUSH FOR GOLD

The discovery of gold in California and Colorado in the middle of the 19th century greatly increased the steady stream of pioneers. One of the most famous routes used by the pioneers was the Oregon Trail, which crossed the continent from Independence, Missouri, through Nebraska, Wyoming, and Idaho to Portland, Oregon, and took six hazardous months to complete. However, danger and hardship did not deter settlers from pushing westward on the trail, lured by the promise of farmland and the chance of finding gold.

Several other wagon trails branched off from the Oregon Trail, including the Mormon Trail to Salt Lake City in Utah. It was established by the Mormons, a Christian sect, to escape persecution in the East. Others included the Central Overland and California trails to San Francisco. Another major trail, the Southern Overland, connected St. Louis with San Francisco via Missouri, Arkansas, Oklahoma, Texas, New Mexico, and Arizona. After gold was found in Montana in 1864, a new route, the Bozeman Trail, branched off from the Oregon Trail to reach these areas.

Many of these old wagon trails exist today as interstate highways. They still follow the paths that Native Americans established over the centuries as the most practical routes across the continent.

SEE ALSO:

- American Revolutionary War
- Cattle Trails
- Ghost Dance
- Hunting
- Indian Territory
- Indian Wars
- Land Rights
- Manifest Destiny
- Movies
- Railroads
- Reservations
- Settlers
- Treaties

Wampum

ABOVE: This wampum belt belonged to the Delaware tribe.

The Algonquian word "wampum" has entered the English language as slang for "money." But for both the Iroquois and the Algonquian it had many uses and meanings.

A wampum is a string of beads that were originally made by grinding down purple and white clamshells. Wampums were used as currency and worn as belts, necklaces, or bracelets. Certain lengths of wampum had specific values, although purple beads were considered to be twice as valuable as white ones.

Ceremony and event-marker

As well as being used for currency, wampums featured prominently in ceremonies. The value of the wampum was related to the richness of the ritual. Wampum was also widely used to maintain a tribal record of agreements. When, for example, the separate Iroquois tribes consolidated and formed the Iroquois League of Five Nations, the event was recorded in symbols on a wampum belt. The belt was held by the Onondaga, the Keepers of the Central Fire, where council meetings of the league were held and where important intertribal decisions were made. Similarly, the agreements made with the Iroquois by William Penn, an English Quaker who founded Pennsylvania, were recorded on a wampum belt.

Wampum belts also functioned as a means of communication between different tribal groups or factions. After the defeat of the French forces in the Great Lakes region Lord Jeffrey Amherst, the British commander-in-chief, granted Seneca tribal lands to his British officers in reward for their services. The Seneca chiefs sent out war belts of wampum to enlist the help of neighboring tribes against the British forces. This act was a precursor to Pontiac's War of 1763.

SEE ALSO:

- Algonquian
- Body Adornment
- Delaware
- French and Indian War
- Iroquois
- Jewelry
- Pontiac's War
- Quillwork and Beadwork
- Treaties

Wovoka

Wovoka was a Paiute preacher and prophet who founded the Ghost Dance movement in 1889. To his followers he was a messiah who heralded destruction for whites and peace and prosperity for all Native Americans.

Wovoka was born in western Nevada in 1856. When he was 14, his father died, and a white rancher called David Wilson took him in. He worked for Wilson, even taking the name Jack Wilson, before falling under the influence of a Pauite shaman called Tavibo.

In 1889 Wovoka had a vision while delirious with a fever. He saw the annihilation of white people and the return of an unfenced North America with huge herds of buffalo. He then started preaching that an era of Native-American supremacy was at hand and encouraged the practice of dancing in circles while singing religious songs to hasten its arrival. The day was fast approaching, he said, when Native Americans would reclaim their lands and be reunited with their ancestors.

Government clampdown

Wovoka's Ghost Dance movement soon spread to the despairing Plains tribespeople, giving them hope after defeats by the U.S. government. His message was spiritual and pacifist, with elements of Christianity, but it raised such expectations of a day of reckoning for the whites that the U.S. feared a rebellion. The government banned the Ghost Dance, but by 1890 many Sioux were performing it every night and calling for an uprising.

ABOVE: Wovoka, the founder of the Ghost Dance movement, was a Southern Paiute of the Walker River Band. He preached that Native Americans should rid themselves of all the white people's ways, especially the use of alcohol.

Inevitably, a U.S. Army clampdown followed, culminating in the tragic massacre at Wounded Knee on December 29, 1890. Wovoka's influence declined after this, and he resumed his former identity as Jack Wilson until his death in 1932.

SEE ALSO:

- Alcohol
- Buffalo
- Ghost Dance
- Paiute
- Plains
- Shamanism
- Sioux
- Wounded Knee

Zuni

Speaking a distinct language unrelated to any other in the Southwest, but possibly with distant links to Tanoan, the Zuni tribe live in a pueblo town in northwestern New Mexico that they have inhabited for at least 600 years. Like the Hopi, Acoma, and Rio Grande Pueblo tribespeople of today, the Zuni are farmers.

The tribe's origins are shrouded in mystery, but it is thought they are descendants of the prehistoric Anasazi, merged with descendants of the Mogollon. They themselves believe they emerged from a sacred place underground. Members of religious cults still hold secret meetings in underground *kivas.*

Seven down to one

When first encountered by the Spanish in the 1500s, the Zuni were living in Hawikuh and a number of other villages—perhaps seven in all. These villages made up the fabled empire of gold, called the Seven Cities of Cibola, that the Spanish conquistador, or conqueror, Francisco de Coronado sought in vain.

The Pueblo Rebellion against the Spanish in 1680 resulted in Spanish atrocities against the Zuni and the tribe's consolidation in the 1690s into one settlement on the site of one of the original villages. But the Zuni's rich cultural and agricultural traditions survive among their 8,000–10,000 members today.

BELOW: Photographed in 1899, these Zuni are taking part in a tribal rain dance.

Fact File

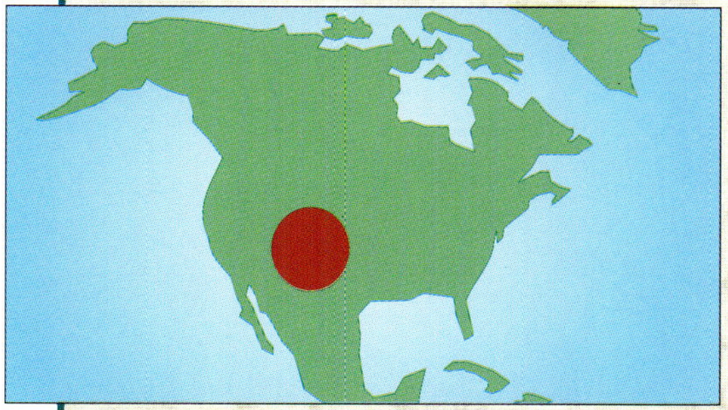

The Zuni tribespeople live in northwestern New Mexico.

LANGUAGE: *Zuni*
AREA: *New Mexico*
RESERVATION: *Northwestern New Mexico, south of Gallup*
POPULATION: *8,000–10,000 today*
HOUSING: *Southwestern adobe (clay brick) houses*
EUROPEAN CONTACT: *Fray Marcos de Niza (Franciscan priest) in 1539*
NEIGHBORS: *Hopi, Navajo, and Acoma*
LIFESTYLE: *Settled farmers*
FOOD: *Corn, peppers, and cornmeal*
CRAFTS: *Carving, jewelry, and pottery*

Traditionally, Zuni men grew a wide variety of corn, peppers, squash, and cotton. They also wove cloth, while women made baskets and pots. Today both men and women produce exquisite jewelry, particularly in silver and turquoise. Such crafts express the traditional Zuni view of the world, which is that people must live in harmony with nature.

Secret male societies

In common with many other tribes in the Southwest, Zuni society is organized into matrilineal clans, with descent passed on through female lines. However, the senior officers in the 13 Zuni clans are all male—as are all the members of the secret religious cults.

Membership in these cults is restricted, and new members have to undergo special initiation ceremonies. The cults organize the complex ceremonial life of the Zuni pueblo. It is based on ancestor worship and impersonations of a variety of gods and supernatural spirits called kachinas—particularly those that bring life-giving rain, such as Sayatasha, Rain Power of the North.

The cults have their own priesthoods and are devoted to the worship of a particular group of gods and other supernatural spirits. For example, during the famous

BELOW: The Zuni are renowned for their jewelry. This bracelet is made of silver, inlaid with mother of pearl, coral, and obsidian.

LEFT: The Zuni, like many Native-American tribes, believed that the eagle was a messenger of the gods. Here a Zuni tribesman poses next to an eagle he has captured. The bird's feathers would have been used to make ceremonial costumes.

Shalako Festival (also called the House Blessing Ceremony), held in early winter, dancers (the Shalakos) move from house to house as they perform. They wear giant masks to represent the messengers of the rain gods coming down from the spirit world to bless new homes. The festival takes 10 months to prepare and lasts for 49 days. It is a reenactment of the Zuni's original emergence from underground and migration to their homeland. The festival is also a time when the spirits of dead ancestors are believed to return to the world to be honored and fed by their living descendants.

SEE ALSO:
- Acoma
- Anasazi
- Basketry
- Clothing
- Corn
- Coronado, Francisco de
- Dance
- Featherwork
- Homes
- Hopi
- Jewelry
- Kachina
- Kiva
- Masks
- Mogollon
- Navajo
- Origin Myths
- Pottery
- Pueblo
- Pueblo Rebellion
- Ritual
- Southwest
- Tanoan Speakers
- Women

A–Z of Native-American Tribes

This A–Z provides a cultural summary of the major Native-American tribes. Where a tribe is the subject of an article in a particular volume of this set, the volume number and page reference are given. Also, alternative historical names for some tribes are shown inside parentheses.

A

ABNAKI (Abenaki)
LANGUAGE: Algonquian
AREA: Northeastern Woodland
HOUSING: Conical bark or mat houses in palisaded villages
NEIGHBORS: Passamaquoddy, Penobscot, Malecite, Micmac
LIFESTYLE: Hunting, fishing, farming
FOOD: Deer, corn, fish
CRAFTS: Quillwork, birchbark, skinwork

ACOMA 1:4
LANGUAGE: Keresan
AREA: Southwest
HOUSING: Multistory adobe
NEIGHBORS: Pueblo, Apache, Navajo, Zuni
LIFESTYLE: Settled farmers
FOOD: Corn, gathered foods, game
CRAFTS: Pottery, weaving

ALEUT (Unangan)
LANGUAGE: Eskimo-Aleut
AREA: Arctic (Aleutian Islands)
HOUSING: Semisubterranean sod- and driftwood-covered shelters
NEIGHBORS: Inuit, Tlingit
LIFESTYLE: Sea-mammal hunting, fishing
FOOD: Seals, shellfish, fish, whales, seabirds, plant foods
CRAFTS: Basketry, ivory carving, gut clothing

APACHE 1:36
LANGUAGE: Athapascan
AREA: Southwest
HOUSING: Brush-covered wickiups, some use of tepees
NEIGHBORS: Pueblo, Navajo, Comanche, Kiowa, Paiute
LIFESTYLE: Nomadic hunting-gathering, some farming
FOOD: Game, roots, berries, some buffalo, some corn
CRAFTS: Basketry, skinwork

ARAPAHO 1:41
LANGUAGE: Algonquian
AREA: Central Plains
HOUSING: Tepees
NEIGHBORS: Cheyenne, Shoshoni, Ute, Kiowa, Pawnee, Sioux
LIFESTYLE: Nomadic hunting
FOOD: Buffalo, deer, roots and berries
CRAFTS: Skin-, bead-, and featherwork

ARIKARA (Ree, Sahnish)
LANGUAGE: Caddoan
AREA: Upper Missouri (Northern Plains)
HOUSING: Earth lodges
NEIGHBORS: Mandan, Hidatsa, Sioux, Pawnee
LIFESTYLE: Some farming, hunting
FOOD: Corn, buffalo, deer, gathered roots and berries
CRAFTS: Skinwork, featherwork

ASSINIBOINE 1:49
LANGUAGE: Siouan
AREA: Northern Plains
HOUSING: Tepees
NEIGHBORS: Blackfoot, Crow, Sioux, Cree
LIFESTYLE: Nomadic hunting
FOOD: Buffalo, deer
CRAFTS: Quill-, bead-, and skinwork

ATHAPASCAN, Northern (Dine or Dene) 1:54
LANGUAGE: Athapascan
AREA: Western Subarctic
HOUSING: Bark-covered wigwams, bark lean-tos, log houses
NEIGHBORS: Inuit, Tlingit, Cree, Blackfoot
LIFESTYLE: Nomadic hunting, fishing, gathering
FOOD: Caribou, wild fowl, fish
CRAFTS: Quillwork, birchbark

B

BELLA BELLA (Heiltsuk)
LANGUAGE: Wakashan
AREA: Northwest Coast
HOUSING: Split cedar plank
NEIGHBORS: Bella Coola, Kwakiutl, Haida, Tsimshian
LIFESTYLE: Sea-mammal hunting, fishing
FOOD: Sea mammals, salmon, shellfish, roots and berries
CRAFTS: Woodcarving

BELLA COOLA (Tallion)
LANGUAGE: Salishan
AREA: Northwest Coast
HOUSING: Split cedar plank
NEIGHBORS: Bella Bella, Kwakiutl, Coast Salish
LIFESTYLE: Sea-mammal hunting, fishing
FOOD: Sea mammals, salmon, shellfish, roots and berries
CRAFTS: Woodcarving

BEOTHUK 2:5
LANGUAGE: Beothukan
AREA: Eastern Subarctic
HOUSING: Birchbark lodges
NEIGHBORS: Inuit, Naskapi, Micmac
LIFESTYLE: Hunting-gathering, fishing
FOOD: Deer, salmon, shellfish, gathered roots and berries
CRAFTS: Woodwork

BLACKFOOT (Siksika, Kainah, Piegan) 2:14
LANGUAGE: Algonquian
AREA: Northern Plains
HOUSING: Tepees
NEIGHBORS: Shoshoni, Crow, Sioux
LIFESTYLE: Nomadic hunting
FOOD: Buffalo, deer
CRAFTS: Quill-, bead-, and skinwork

C

CADDO Confederacy (Kadohadacho) 2:38
LANGUAGE: Caddoan
AREA: Southern Plains
HOUSING: Domed thatched houses
NEIGHBORS: Choctaw, Chickasaw, Wichita
LIFESTYLE: Farming and hunting
FOOD: Buffalo, deer, corn
CRAFTS: Woodcarving, basketry

CALUSA
LANGUAGE: Muskogean
AREA: Southern Florida
HOUSING: Palm-thatched shelters
NEIGHBORS: Timucua
LIFESTYLE: Fishing, hunting
FOOD: Fish, shellfish
CRAFTS: Woodcarving

CAYUSE
LANGUAGE: Penutian
AREA: Plateau
HOUSING: Rush mat-covered lodges, some use of tepees
NEIGHBORS: Shoshoni, Nez Percé, Flathead
LIFESTYLE: Hunting, fishing
FOOD: Deer, salmon, roots and berries
CRAFTS: Basketry, skinwork

CHEROKEE (Tsaragi)
LANGUAGE: Iroquoian
AREA: Southeast
HOUSING: Palisaded townships of log cabins
NEIGHBORS: Creek, Catawba
LIFESTYLE: Farming, some hunting
FOOD: Corn, beans, squash
CRAFTS: Woodcarving, basketry

CHEYENNE 2:56
LANGUAGE: Algonquian
AREA: Central Plains
HOUSING: Tepees
NEIGHBORS: Shoshoni, Arapaho, Sioux
LIFESTYLE: Nomadic hunting
FOOD: Buffalo, deer, gathered roots and berries
CRAFTS: Skin-, bead-, and featherwork

CHICKASAW
LANGUAGE: Muskogean
AREA: Southeast
HOUSING: Palisaded townships
NEIGHBORS: Choctaw, Caddo, Natchez, Creek
LIFESTYLE: Farming, some hunting
FOOD: Corn, beans, squash
CRAFTS: Basketry

CHINOOK (Tsi-Nuk) 3:4
LANGUAGE: Chinookan
AREA: Southern Northwest Coast
HOUSING: Semisubterranean split-plank houses
NEIGHBORS: Coast Salish, Klikitat
LIFESTYLE: Trading, fishing
FOOD: Salmon, game animals, gathered roots and berries
CRAFTS: Woodcarving

CHOCTAW (Chata)
LANGUAGE: Muskogean
AREA: Southeast
HOUSING: Palisaded townships
NEIGHBORS: Natchez, Chickasaw, Creek
LIFESTYLE: Farming, fishing, hunting
FOOD: Corn, beans, deer, birds, turtles, fish, nuts and berries
CRAFTS: Split-cane basketry

CHUGACH
LANGUAGE: Inuit
AREA: Western Arctic
HOUSING: Sod- and driftwood-covered lodges
NEIGHBORS: Tlingit, Northern Athapascan
LIFESTYLE: Sea-mammal hunting, hunting, fishing
FOOD: Sea mammals, shellfish, fish, caribou
CRAFTS: Ivory carving

CHUMASH 3:7
LANGUAGE: Chumashan (Hokan)
AREA: California
HOUSING: Thatched huts
NEIGHBORS: Mission Tribes, Yokut
LIFESTYLE: Sea-mammal hunting, fishing, gathering
FOOD: Sea mammals, shellfish, fish, plants and berries
CRAFTS: Shellwork, stonework, basketry

COAST SALISH 3:15
LANGUAGE: Salishan
AREA: Southern Northwest Coast
HOUSING: Split-plank houses
NEIGHBORS: Kwakiutl, Chinook
LIFESTYLE: Fishing, sea-mammal hunting
FOOD: Salmon, shellfish, seal, sea birds, roots and berries
CRAFTS: Woodcarving

COMANCHE 3:20
LANGUAGE: Uto-Aztecan
AREA: Southern Plains
HOUSING: Tepees
NEIGHBORS: Kiowa, Apache
LIFESTYLE: Nomadic hunting
FOOD: Buffalo, other game, gathered roots and berries
CRAFTS: Skinwork, beadwork

CREE (Knistenaux) 3:38
LANGUAGE: Algonquian
AREA: Subarctic
HOUSING: Bark-covered wigwams
NEIGHBORS: Athapascan, Inuit, Blackfoot, Ojibway
LIFESTYLE: Nomadic hunting-gathering, trapping, fishing
FOOD: Game animals, fish, gathered roots and berries
CRAFTS: Birchbark, quillwork, beadwork

CREEK (Muskogee)
LANGUAGE: Muskogean
AREA: Southeast
HOUSING: Palisaded townships
NEIGHBORS: Choctaw, Chickasaw, Cherokee, Timucua
LIFESTYLE: Farming
FOOD: Corn, beans, squash, game
CRAFTS: Cane basketry, silverwork

CROW (Apsaroke) 3:42
LANGUAGE: Siouan
AREA: Northern Plains
HOUSING: Tepees
NEIGHBORS: Blackfoot, Assiniboine, Sioux
LIFESTYLE: Nomadic hunting
FOOD: Buffalo, deer, gathered roots and berries
CRAFTS: Skin-, bead-, and featherwork

D

DELAWARE (Leni Lenape) 3:56
LANGUAGE: Algonquian
AREA: Eastern Woodland
HOUSING: Palisaded villages of bark lodges
NEIGHBORS: Iroquois, Woodland Algonquian
LIFESTYLE: Farming, hunting
FOOD: Corn, game, fish, gathered plants and berries
CRAFTS: Woodcarving, beadwork

F

FLATHEAD
LANGUAGE: Salishan
AREA: Plateau
HOUSING: Semisubterranean earth- or brush-covered pit houses
NEIGHBORS: Cayuse, Coeur D'Alene, Nez Percé
LIFESTYLE: Fishing, gathering, hunting
FOOD: Salmon, buffalo, deer, roots and berries
CRAFTS: Basketry, beadwork

G

GROS VENTRE (Atsina)
LANGUAGE: Algonquian
AREA: Northern Plains
HOUSING: Tepees
NEIGHBORS: Blackfoot, Crow, Assiniboine, Sioux
LIFESTYLE: Nomadic hunting
FOOD: Buffalo, deer, gathered roots and berries
CRAFTS: Beadwork, skinwork

H

HAIDA 4:43
LANGUAGE: Haida (distant link to Athapascan)
AREA: Northwest Coast
HOUSING: Split cedar plank
NEIGHBORS: Tlingit, Tsimshian
LIFESTYLE: Sea-mammal hunting, fishing
FOOD: Salmon, sea mammals, seabirds, some plant foods
CRAFTS: Woodcarving, basketry, argillite (a type of rock) carving

HIDATSA (Minnetaree)
LANGUAGE: Siouan
AREA: Northern Plains
HOUSING: Earth-lodge villages
NEIGHBORS: Mandan, Arikara, Sioux
LIFESTYLE: Farming, seasonal buffalo hunting
FOOD: Corn, beans, squash, vegetables, buffalo
CRAFTS: Skinwork, beadwork

HITCHITI
LANGUAGE: Muskogean
AREA: Southeast
HOUSING: Palisaded villages
NEIGHBORS: Creek, Cherokee
LIFESTYLE: Farming, some hunting
FOOD: Corn, beans, squash, game
CRAFTS: Basketry

HOPI (Moki) 4:50
LANGUAGE: Uto-Aztecan
AREA: Southwest
HOUSING: Multistory adobe
NEIGHBORS: Pueblo tribes, Navajo, Apache
LIFESTYLE: Farming
FOOD: Corn, beans, squash
CRAFTS: Weaving, basketry, woodwork

HUPA 4:61
LANGUAGE: Athapascan
AREA: Northern California
HOUSING: Cedar plank houses
NEIGHBORS: Yurok, Karok, Pomo
LIFESTYLE: Fishing, hunting, gathering
FOOD: Salmon, shellfish, acorns, game, roots and berries
CRAFTS: Shell engraving, fiber weaving, basketry, featherwork

HURON (Wendat, Wyandot, Tobacco) 4:62
LANGUAGE: Iroquoian
AREA: Northeast Woodland
HOUSING: Palisaded villages of bark-covered longhouses
NEIGHBORS: Ojibway, Potawatomi, Iroquois
LIFESTYLE: Farming, some hunting
FOOD: Corn, beans, squash, deer, gathered plant foods
CRAFTS: Quillwork, splint basketry, fiber weaving

I

INGALIK
LANGUAGE: Athapascan
AREA: Arctic
HOUSING: Brush, bark, and driftwood shelters
NEIGHBORS: Inuit, Tlingit
LIFESTYLE: Fishing, hunting
FOOD: Salmon, caribou, moose, waterfowl, roots and berries
CRAFTS: Skinwork, woodcarving, basketry

INUIT (Eskimo) 5:14
LANGUAGE: Inuit
AREA: Arctic
HOUSING: Snow houses (igloos), whalebone and driftwood shelters
NEIGHBORS: Northern Athapascan, Tlingit, Cree
LIFESTYLE: Nomadic hunting and fishing
FOOD: Sea mammals, whales, fish, caribou, some gathered foods
CRAFTS: Ivory carving

IOWA
LANGUAGE: Siouan
AREA: Eastern Plains
HOUSING: Dome-shaped earth lodges, tepees when hunting
NEIGHBORS: Sioux, Omaha, Oto
LIFESTYLE: Farming, seasonal buffalo hunting
FOOD: Corn, buffalo, deer, some gathered foods
CRAFTS: Skinwork, beadwork, some carved stonework

IROQUOIS Confederacy (Five Nations, Six Nations) 5:20
LANGUAGE: Iroquoian
AREA: Northeast Woodland
HOUSING: Stockaded villages of elm-bark-covered longhouses
NEIGHBORS: Huron, Ojibway, Northeast Woodland Algonquian
LIFESTYLE: Farming, some hunting and fishing
FOOD: Corn, beans, squash, maple syrup, nuts, roots, deer
CRAFTS: Skinwork, splint baskets, woodwork, shellwork

K

KANSA (Kaw)
LANGUAGE: Siouan
AREA: Eastern Plains
HOUSING: Dome-shaped earth lodges, tepees when hunting
NEIGHBORS: Pawnee, Oto, Osage
LIFESTYLE: Farming, seasonal buffalo hunting
FOOD: Corn, beans, buffalo, deer
CRAFTS: Skinwork, beadwork

KAROK
LANGUAGE: Karok (Hokan)
AREA: Northern California
HOUSING: Plank houses
NEIGHBORS: Yurok, Modoc, Hupa
LIFESTYLE: Fishing, hunting, gathering
FOOD: Salmon, other fish, acorns, gathered roots and berries
CRAFTS: Basketry, shellwork, featherwork

KICKAPOO (Kiwigapaw)
LANGUAGE: Algonquian
AREA: Great Lakes
HOUSING: Bark lodges in semi-permanent villages
NEIGHBORS: Sauk and Fox, Potawatomi, Winnebago
LIFESTYLE: Hunting, farming, gathering
FOOD: Game, fish, corn, wild rice
CRAFTS: Barkwork, beadwork, woven bags

KIOWA 5:37
LANGUAGE: Tanoan
AREA: Southern Plains
HOUSING: Tepees
NEIGHBORS: Comanche, Wichita, Kansa
LIFESTYLE: Nomadic buffalo hunting
FOOD: Buffalo, deer, gathered roots and berries
CRAFTS: Skin-, bead-, and featherwork

KIOWA-APACHE
LANGUAGE: Athapascan
AREA: Southern Plains
HOUSING: Tepees
NEIGHBORS: Kiowa, Comanche
LIFESTYLE: Nomadic buffalo hunting
FOOD: Buffalo, deer, gathered roots and berries
CRAFTS: Skin-, bead-, and featherwork

KLAMATH 5:42
LANGUAGE: Klamath
AREA: Northern California
HOUSING: Plank houses
NEIGHBORS: Takelma, Yurok, Karok
LIFESTYLE: Fishing, hunting
FOOD: Salmon, acorns, game, gathered roots and berries
CRAFTS: Basketry, some shell- and woodwork

KUTCHIN (Loucheux)
LANGUAGE: Athapascan
AREA: Western Subarctic
HOUSING: Skin wigwams, log houses
NEIGHBORS: Northern Athapascan, Inuit
LIFESTYLE: Hunting, fishing, gathering
FOOD: Caribou, moose, salmon, herring, roots and berries
CRAFTS: Skinwork, beadwork

KUTENAI
LANGUAGE: Kutenai
AREA: Plateau
HOUSING: Bark- and mat-covered
NEIGHBORS: Pend D'Oreille, Nez Percé
LIFESTYLE: Hunting, fishing, gathering
FOOD: Buffalo, deer, fish, gathered roots and berries
CRAFTS: Basketry, beadwork

KWAKIUTL 5:44
LANGUAGE: Wakashan
AREA: Northwest Coast
HOUSING: Split cedar plank
NEIGHBORS: Nootka, Coast Salish
LIFESTYLE: Sea-mammal hunting, fishing
FOOD: Salmon, sea mammals, shellfish, roots and berries
CRAFTS: Woodcarving, basketry

M

MAIDU
LANGUAGE: Maidu (Penutian)
AREA: Northern California
HOUSING: Earth-covered lodges
NEIGHBORS: Pomo, Miwok
LIFESTYLE: Fishing, gathering
FOOD: Fish, acorns, game, gathered roots and berries
CRAFTS: Basketry, featherwork

MANDAN (Mihwatoni)
LANGUAGE: Siouan
AREA: Northern Plains
HOUSING: Stockaded villages of domed earth lodges
NEIGHBORS: Hidatsa, Arikara, Sioux
LIFESTYLE: Farming, seasonal buffalo hunting
FOOD: Corn, beans, buffalo, deer, roots and berries
CRAFTS: Skinwork, beadwork

MENOMINEE
LANGUAGE: Algonquian
AREA: Great Lakes
HOUSING: Semipermanent bark lodge villages
NEIGHBORS: Winnebago, Sauk and Fox
LIFESTYLE: Hunting, farming, fishing
FOOD: Corn, wild rice, game, roots and berries
CRAFTS: Woodwork, woven bags, quillwork

MICMAC 6:29
LANGUAGE: Algonquian
AREA: Northeast Woodland
HOUSING: Bark and grass mat-covered wigwams
NEIGHBORS: Beothuk, Northeast Woodland Algonquian
LIFESTYLE: Hunting, fishing
FOOD: Fish, shellfish, moose, caribou, waterfowl, plant foods
CRAFTS: Quillwork, birchbark

MISSION INDIANS 6:33
LANGUAGE: Mainly Uto-Aztecan and Hokan
AREA: Southern California
HOUSING: Thatch shelters
NEIGHBORS: Chumash, Mohave, Yuma
LIFESTYLE: Fishing, gathering
FOOD: Fish, shellfish, acorns, rodents, roots and berries
CRAFTS: Basketry

MODOC 6:42
LANGUAGE: Penutian
AREA: Northern California
HOUSING: Plank houses
NEIGHBORS: Yurok, Karok, Hupa
LIFESTYLE: Fishing, hunting, gathering
FOOD: Fish, shellfish, deer, gathered plants and berries
CRAFTS: Beadwork, basketry

MOHAVE (Mojave)
LANGUAGE: Hokan
AREA: Southwest
HOUSING: Domed thatch houses, sometimes covered with sand
NEIGHBORS: Yuma, Apache, Pima, Papago
LIFESTYLE: Hunting, fishing, gathering
FOOD: Deer, fish, gathered roots and berries
CRAFTS: Beadwork, pottery dolls, bark weaving

MOHEGAN 6:50
LANGUAGE: Algonquian
AREA: Eastern Woodland
HOUSING: Villages of bark-covered houses
NEIGHBORS: Iroquois, Northeast Woodland Algonquian
LIFESTYLE: Farming, hunting
FOOD: Corn, beans, deer, gathered roots and berries
CRAFTS: Basketry

MONTAGNAIS
LANGUAGE: Algonquian
AREA: Eastern Subarctic
HOUSING: Birchbark-covered wigwams
NEIGHBORS: Naskapi, Cree
LIFESTYLE: Hunting
FOOD: Caribou, moose, gathered plant foods, some fish
CRAFTS: Skinwork, birchbark

N

NASKAPI 7:4
LANGUAGE: Algonquian
AREA: Eastern Subarctic
HOUSING: Birchbark-covered wigwams
NEIGHBORS: Montagnais, Cree, Inuit
LIFESTYLE: Hunting, fishing, some gathering
FOOD: Caribou, moose, waterfowl, some gathered plant foods
CRAFTS: Caribou skinwork, birchbark

NATCHEZ (Avoyel) 7:6
LANGUAGE: Natchez
AREA: Southeast
HOUSING: Palisaded townships, thatched cabins on earth mounds
NEIGHBORS: Caddo, Chickasaw, Choctaw
LIFESTYLE: Farming, some hunting
FOOD: Corn, sunflowers, melons, deer, some gathered foods
CRAFTS: Basketry, weaving

NAVAJO (Dine or Dene) 7:9
LANGUAGE: Athapascan
AREA: Southwest
HOUSING: Hogans
NEIGHBORS: Apache, Pueblo
LIFESTYLE: Seminomadic hunting and gathering, herding, farming

FOOD: Small game, gathered roots and berries, corn
CRAFTS: Weaving, silverwork

NEZ PERCÉ (Chute-Pa-Lu) 7:13
LANGUAGE: Penutian
AREA: Plateau
HOUSING: Cattail mat multifamily houses, some tepees
NEIGHBORS: Flathead, Cayuse, Shoshoni
LIFESTYLE: Fishing, hunting, gathering
FOOD: Salmon, buffalo, deer, gathered roots and berries
CRAFTS: Basketry, woven bags, skinwork, beadwork

NOOTKA (Nuu-Chah-Nulth) 7:19
LANGUAGE: Wakashan
AREA: Northwest Coast
HOUSING: Split cedar plank
NEIGHBORS: Coast Salish, Kwakiutl
LIFESTYLE: Sea-mammal hunting, whaling, fishing
FOOD: Seals, whales, salmon, shellfish, roots and berries
CRAFTS: Woodcarving, basketry, some shellwork

O

OJIBWAY (CHIPPEWA; also Saulteaux, Flambeaux, Pillagers, Anishinabe) 7:24
LANGUAGE: Algonquian
AREA: Great Lakes
HOUSING: Large villages of bark-covered wigwams
NEIGHBORS: Cree, Ottawa, Iroquois
LIFESTYLE: Farming, hunting, fishing, gathering
FOOD: Caribou, moose, fish, wild rice, maple syrup, fruits
CRAFTS: Basketry, birchbark, woodcarving, rush weaving

OMAHA
LANGUAGE: Siouan
AREA: Eastern Plains
HOUSING: Earth lodge villages, tepees when hunting
NEIGHBORS: Pawnee, Sioux, Iowa, Oto
LIFESTYLE: Farming, seasonal buffalo hunting
FOOD: Corn, buffalo, deer, gathered plant foods
CRAFTS: Skinwork, beadwork, ribbon appliqué

OSAGE 7:32
LANGUAGE: Siouan
AREA: Eastern Plains
HOUSING: Earth lodge villages, tepees when hunting
NEIGHBORS: Pawnee, Kiowa, Caddo
LIFESTYLE: Farming, seasonal buffalo hunting
FOOD: Corn, buffalo, deer, gathered plant foods
CRAFTS: Skinwork, beadwork, ribbon appliqué

OTO
LANGUAGE: Siouan
AREA: Eastern Plains
HOUSING: Earth lodge villages, tepees when hunting
NEIGHBORS: Pawnee, Osage, Sioux
LIFESTYLE: Farming, seasonal buffalo hunting
FOOD: Corn, buffalo, deer, gathered plant foods
CRAFTS: Skinwork, beadwork

OTTAWA
LANGUAGE: Algonquian
AREA: Great Lakes
HOUSING: Villages of bark-covered wigwams
NEIGHBORS: Ojibway, Cree, Iroquois
LIFESTYLE: Farming, fishing, hunting, gathering
FOOD: Wild rice, fish, game, gathered roots and berries
CRAFTS: Quillwork, birchbark

P

PAIUTE (Chemehuevi) 7:36
LANGUAGE: Uto-Aztecan
AREA: Great Basin
HOUSING: Brush-covered wickiups, some use of tepees
NEIGHBORS: Ute, Shoshoni
LIFESTYLE: Nomadic hunting and gathering
FOOD: Small game, birds, roots and berries, insects, reptiles
CRAFTS: Basketry, rabbitskin blankets

PAPAGO (Tohono-O-Otam) 7:45
LANGUAGE: Uto-Aztecan
AREA: Southwest
HOUSING: Thatched wickiups
NEIGHBORS: Pima, Apache, Mohave
LIFESTYLE: Farming, hunting, gathering, fishing
FOOD: Corn, beans, squash, deer, roots and berries, some fish
CRAFTS: Basketry

PAWNEE (Skidi, Kitkehaxki, Pitahaurata, Chaui) 7:49
LANGUAGE: Caddoan
AREA: Eastern Plains
HOUSING: Earth lodge villages
NEIGHBORS: Sioux, Arapaho, Kiowa, Osage
LIFESTYLE: Farming, seasonal buffalo hunting
FOOD: Corn, beans, squash, buffalo, deer, roots and berries
CRAFTS: Skinwork, beadwork

PEQUOT
LANGUAGE: Algonquian
AREA: Eastern Woodland
HOUSING: Stockaded towns of bark-covered lodges
NEIGHBORS: Northeast Woodland Algonquian
LIFESTYLE: Farming, some hunting and gathering
FOOD: Corn, beans, squash, deer, gathered roots and berries
CRAFTS: Quillwork, beadwork

PIMA (Ah-Kee-Mult-O-O-Tam) 7:45
LANGUAGE: Uto-Aztecan
AREA: Southwest
HOUSING: Thatched wickiups
NEIGHBORS: Papago, Apache, Mohave
LIFESTYLE: Farming, hunting, gathering, fishing
FOOD: Corn, beans, squash, deer, roots, berries, mesquite, fish
CRAFTS: Basketry

POMO 7:60
LANGUAGE: Pomo (Hokan)
AREA: Central California
HOUSING: Tule-covered lodges
NEIGHBORS: Hupa, Wintun, Miwok
LIFESTYLE: Hunting, fishing, gathering
FOOD: Game, fish, acorns, gathered roots and berries
CRAFTS: Basketry, featherwork

PONCA
LANGUAGE: Siouan
AREA: Eastern Plains
HOUSING: Villages of earth lodges, tepees when hunting
NEIGHBORS: Sioux, Pawnee, Omaha
LIFESTYLE: Farming, seasonal buffalo hunting
FOOD: Corn, vegetables, buffalo, deer, gathered roots and berries
CRAFTS: Skinwork, beadwork

POTAWATOMI
LANGUAGE: Algonquian
AREA: Northeast Woodland
HOUSING: Bark-covered lodges
NEIGHBORS: Sauk and Fox, Kickapoo, Iroquois
LIFESTYLE: Farming, fishing, some hunting and gathering
FOOD: Corn, fish, deer, wild plants and roots
CRAFTS: Beadwork, ribbon appliqué, birchbark

POWHATAN Confederacy
LANGUAGE: Algonquian
AREA: Eastern Woodland
HOUSING: Palisaded villages of thatch- or bark-covered lodges
NEIGHBORS: Northeast Woodland Algonquian
LIFESTYLE: Farming, some hunting and gathering
FOOD: Corn, beans, squash, deer, gathered plant foods
CRAFTS: Beadwork

PUEBLO 8:17
LANGUAGE: Tanoan and Keresan
AREA: Southwest
HOUSING: Multistory adobe
NEIGHBORS: Apache, Navajo
LIFESTYLE: Farming, some hunting
FOOD: Corn, beans, squash, deer, gathered roots and berries
CRAFTS: Pottery, silverwork, weaving

S

SALISH 8:57
LANGUAGE: Salishan
AREA: Plateau
HOUSING: Semisubterranean brush- or earth-covered lodges
NEIGHBORS: Blackfoot, Nez Percé, Cayuse
LIFESTYLE: Fishing, hunting, trapping, and gathering
FOOD: Salmon, river fish, deer, wild roots and berries
CRAFTS: Basketry

SAUK and FOX (Sac, Mesquakie) 8:63
LANGUAGE: Algonquian
AREA: Great Lakes
HOUSING: Bark-covered lodges, tepees when hunting
NEIGHBORS: Kickapoo, Sioux
LIFESTYLE: Farming, gathering, trapping, seasonal hunting
FOOD: Corn, beans, squash, wild rice, buffalo, roots and berries
CRAFTS: Quillwork, woven bags, ribbon appliqué

SEMINOLE 9:7
LANGUAGE: Muskogean
AREA: Florida
HOUSING: Palm-thatched chickees raised on stilts
NEIGHBORS: Miccosukee
LIFESTYLE: Fishing, hunting, farming
FOOD: Corn, beans, shellfish, fish, roots
CRAFTS: Ribbon patchwork

SHAWNEE 9:22
LANGUAGE: Algonquian
AREA: Southeast
HOUSING: Palisaded townships
NEIGHBORS: Kickapoo, Creek
LIFESTYLE: Farming, some hunting
FOOD: Corn, deer, gathered roots and berries
CRAFTS: Beadwork, some pottery

SHOSHONI (Tsosoni)
LANGUAGE: Uto-Aztecan
AREA: Western Plains
HOUSING: Brush-covered wickiups, tepees
NEIGHBORS: Blackfoot, Cheyenne, Arapaho, Ute, Paiute
LIFESTYLE: Nomadic hunting and gathering
FOOD: Buffalo in East, wild plant foods in West
CRAFTS: Skinwork, beadwork

SIOUX (Dakota, Lakota, Nakota) 9:27
LANGUAGE: Siouan
AREA: Northern and Eastern Plains
HOUSING: Tepees
NEIGHBORS: Blackfoot, Crow, Cheyenne, Arapaho, Winnebago
LIFESTYLE: Nomadic hunting and gathering
FOOD: Buffalo, deer, wild plants
CRAFTS: Skinwork, beadwork

T

TAOS (Tua) 9:51
LANGUAGE: Tanoan
AREA: Southwest
HOUSING: Multistory adobe
NEIGHBORS: Pueblo tribes, Apache, Navajo
LIFESTYLE: Farming
FOOD: Corn, beans, squash, some game, gathered foods
CRAFTS: Pottery, some basketry

TIMUCUA (Utina) 9:59
LANGUAGE: Timucuan (related to Muskogean)
AREA: Florida
HOUSING: Villages of palm-thatched houses
NEIGHBORS: Calusa, Apalachee
LIFESTYLE: Farming, hunting, fishing
FOOD: Corn, beans, fish, birds, alligators, plant foods
CRAFTS: Pottery

TLINGIT 9:61
LANGUAGE: Tlingit (related to Athapascan)
AREA: Northern Northwest Coast
HOUSING: Split cedar plank
NEIGHBORS: Tsimshian, Chugach, Inuit, Northern Athapascan
LIFESTYLE: Trading, sea-mammal hunting, fishing
FOOD: Salmon, other fish, sea mammals, shellfish
CRAFTS: Woodcarving, basketry, weaving

TSIMSHIAN 10:23
LANGUAGE: Chimmesyan (related to Penutian)
AREA: Northwest Coast
HOUSING: Split cedar plank
NEIGHBORS: Tlingit, Haida, Bella Bella
LIFESTYLE: Trading, sea-mammal hunting, fishing
FOOD: Salmon, other fish, sea mammals, shellfish
CRAFTS: Woodcarving, basketry

U

UTE (Nunt'z)
LANGUAGE: Uto-Aztecan
AREA: Great Basin
HOUSING: Brush-covered wickiups
NEIGHBORS: Paiute, Shoshoni, Navajo
LIFESTYLE: Nomadic gathering
FOOD: Small game, reptiles, insects, plants, roots and berries
CRAFTS: Basketry, beadwork

W

WICHITA
LANGUAGE: Caddoan
AREA: Southern Plains
HOUSING: Domed thatched houses
NEIGHBORS: Kiowa, Comanche, Caddo Confederacy
LIFESTYLE: Farming, hunting

FOOD: Corn, buffalo, deer, gathered roots and berries
CRAFTS: Skinwork, beadwork

WINNEBAGO
LANGUAGE: Siouan
AREA: Great Lakes
HOUSING: Earth- or bark-covered houses, tepees when hunting
NEIGHBORS: Sauk and Fox, Potawatomi
LIFESTYLE: Farming, seasonal hunting
FOOD: Corn, buffalo, deer, wild rice, fish, roots and berries
CRAFTS: Pottery, skin-, quill- and beadwork

WINTUN
LANGUAGE: Wintun (Penutian)
AREA: Central California
HOUSING: Mat-covered lodges
NEIGHBORS: Pomo, Maidu
LIFESTYLE: Hunting, fishing, gathering
FOOD: Salmon, deer, acorns, gathered roots and berries
CRAFTS: Basketry, featherwork, some woodwork

Y

YAQUI
LANGUAGE: Uto-Aztecan
AREA: Southwest
HOUSING: Villages of thatched lodges
NEIGHBORS: Pima, Papago, Apache
LIFESTYLE: Farming, hunting, gathering
FOOD: Corn, small game, gathered roots and berries
CRAFTS: Skinwork, some woodcarving

YUMA (Quechan)
LANGUAGE: Hokan
AREA: Southwest
HOUSING: Thatched lodges
NEIGHBORS: Mohave, Papago, Pima, Apache
LIFESTYLE: Farming, hunting, gathering
FOOD: Corn, melons, deer, gathered roots and berries
CRAFTS: Beadwork, pottery dolls

YUROK (Weitspekan)
LANGUAGE: Yurok
AREA: Northern California
HOUSING: Driftwood or plank
NEIGHBORS: Klamath, Karok, Modoc
LIFESTYLE: Hunting, fishing, gathering
FOOD: Deer, fish, roots and berries
CRAFTS: Shellwork, basketry

Z

ZUNI (A'shiwi) 10:62
LANGUAGE: Zunian
AREA: Southwest
HOUSING: Multistory adobe
NEIGHBORS: Pueblo, Apache, Navajo
LIFESTYLE: Farming, some hunting
FOOD: Corn, beans, squash, small game, some gathered plants
CRAFTS: Pottery, weaving, woodcarving, silverwork

FURTHER READING

Calloway, C. G. *New Worlds for All: Indians, Europeans, and the Remaking of Early America.* Baltimore, MD: Johns Hopkins University Press, 1997.

Edmonds, S. and P. Kernaghan. *Native Peoples of North America: Diversity and Development.* New York: Cambridge University Press, 1994.

Hirschfelder, A., ed. *Nature Heritage: Personal Accounts by American Indians, 1790 to the Present.* New York: Macmillan, General Reference, 1995.

Hoxie, F. E. *Encyclopedia of North American Indians.* Boston, MA: Houghton Mifflin Co., 1996.

Hyslop, S. G. and H. Woodhead, eds. *Chroniclers of Indian Life.* Alexandria, VA: Time Life, 1996.

Johnson, M. G. and R. Hook. *The Native Tribes of North America: A Concise Encyclopedia.* New York: Macmillan, 1994.

Josephy, A. M. *500 Nations: An Illustrated History of North American Indians.* New York: Knopf, 1998.

Keller, R. H. and M. F. Turek. *American Indians and National Parks.* Tuscon, AZ: University of Arizona Press, 1998.

Long, A. and M. Boldt. *Governments in Conflict: Provinces and Indian Nations in Canada.* Toronto, Ontario: University of Toronto Press, 1998.

Maynard, J., ed. *Through Indian Eyes: The Untold Story of Native American Peoples.* Pleasantville, NY: Readers Digest, 1996.

Meltzer, D. J. *Search for the First Americans.* Washington, DC: Smithsonian Books, 1995.

Miller, L., ed. *From the Heart: Voices of the American Indian.* New York: Knopf, 1995.

Nichols, R. L. *Indians in the United States and Canada: A Comparative History.* Lincoln, NE: University of Nebraska Press, 1998.

Pritzker, B. *Native Americans: An Encyclopedia of History, Culture, and Peoples.* Santa Barbara, CA: ABC-Clio, 1998.

Sperber, C. and A. J. Joffe. *The First Immigrants from Asia: A Population History of the North American Indians.* New York: Plenum Publishing Corporation, 1992.

Steele, I. K. *Warpaths: Invasions of North America.* New York: Oxford University Press, 1994.

Thornton, R., ed. *Studying Native America: Problems and Prospects.* Madison, WI: University of Wisconsin Press, 1999.

Trigger, B. G. and W. E. Washburn, eds. *The Cambridge History of the Native Peoples of the Americas: North America.* New York: Cambridge University Press, 1996.

Turner, G. *Indians of North America.* New York: Sterling Publications, 1992.

Waldrum, C. and M. Braun. *Atlas of the North American Indian.* New York: Facts on File, 1995.

Warhus, M. *Another America: Native American Maps and the History of Our Land.* New York: St. Martin's Press, 1997.

SET INDEX

Volume numbers and page numbers for main entries are shown in **bold**. Page numbers of illustrations or picture captions are shown in *italic*. Additional references can be found in the SEE ALSOs at the ends of the main entries.

A

Abnaki **5:32**, 35, 36, **8**:27
Acadia **8**:27
Acoma tribe 1:4–5, 6, **8**:10, 17
Acoma village 1:*4*, **6**, **8**:18
acorns **2**:44, **4**:27, 58, **6**:33–4, **7**:60
Adams–Onis Treaty (1819) **9**:11
Adena and Hopewell 1:7–8, **8**:47, **9**:*14*, 15, 64, **10**:12
see also Serpent Mound
adobe **1**:15, **4**:49, **6**:14, 48, **8**:21
adulthood **3**:61–2
see also Vision Quest
afterlife 1:9–11, **3**:54–5
agriculture 1:12–15, **4**:26–7, 38
and Algonquian-speakers **1**:22
and the Allotment Act **1**:26
and the Anasazi **1**:35
ceremonies **3**:*25*, **4**:22–3, **8**:45
and the Huron **4**:63
"Three Sisters" crops **5**:20
see also corn; irrigation
AIM *see* American Indian Movement
Ais **6**:64, **9**:59
Alaska, and the Russians **8**:50–1, **9**:61
Alaska Native Claims Settlement Act **9**:61
Alcatraz Island, occupation of (1969) **7**:42–4
alcohol 1:16–17
Aleut **1**:43, **3**:*50*, **4**:20, **5**:14, 18
clothing **3**:12–13
and the Russians **8**:51
Algonquian speakers 1:21–4, **10**:56–7, 57
birchbark **2**:8
religion **6**:19
reservations **1**:24
rivaling the Iroquois **1**:23
Subarctic **1**:45, **2**:5
Three Fires Confederacy **2**:9
trade and settlers **1**:23
see also French and Indian War; Pontiac's War
Algonquian tribal group 1:18–20
and European wars **1**:19–20
shell-money **5**:26
tribal conflicts **1**:20
see also Midewiwin; Naskapi; Powhatan Wars
Alien Registration Act (1940) **5**:*53*
Alights on the Cloud **3**:35
Allotment Act (1887) **1:25–6**, **3**:60, **5**:8, **7**:51, **9**:10, 18
alphabet, Cherokee **9**:13
American Civil War 1:27–30, **7**:33, 47
American Fur Company **1**:49, **2**:17, **4**:32
American Indian Movement (AIM) **6**:17, **7**:42, 43–4, **9**:30, **10**:22
American Indian Policy Review Commission **10**:22
American Indian Religious Freedom Act (1978) **8**:56
American Revolutionary War 1:31–3, **4**:*23*, **10**:13
and the Creek **6**:64
and the Iroquois **1**:*32–3*, **2**:30–1
and land **8**:40
and the Mohawk **1**:32, **2**:*31*, **6**:49
and the Shawnee **1**:33, **9**:23
Amherst, Jeffrey **7**:63, 64, **10**:40
Anasazi 1:15, **34–5**, **4**:*9*, **6**:24, **8**:17–18, **9**:37, 64, **10**:62
at Canyon de Chelly **2**:49, *50*, **8**:*17*
at Chaco Canyon **2**:*54*–5, **8**:22
highways **2**:55
and the Mogollon **6**:47–8
pottery **1**:34, *35*, **2**:*50*, **8**:10
Animal Masters **3**:25
animals
charms from **1**:*54*
power from **3**:*44*, **9**:24–5
respect for **1**:52, **3**:31, 33, 53, **9**:49, 62
spirits **1**:52, **4**:26, *59*, **6**:21, 32, **9**:24–*5*, 49, **10**:47
see also hunting
Antelope House **2**:50
Apache 1:36–40, 54, **9**:4, 39
and alcohol **1**:16
girls **3**:62
gods **1**:*40*, **9**:*39*
language **1**:55
military chiefs *see* Cochise; Geronimo; Mangas Coloradas
music **6**:61
puberty ritual **1**:40, **8**:46
scouts **9**:5
shields **9**:24–5
taboos **9**:49
war parties **3**:53–4
warriors **3**:*16*, *17*, **4**:**12**, **9**:*39*, **10**:47
Apache Trail **6**:*4*
Apalachee **8**:27, **9**:59
Applegate Trail **6**:44
Arapaho 1:41–2, **2**:53, **3**:*34*, **4**:*12*, *42*, **5**:37, **7**:54
marriage **6**:6
reservations **1**:41, 42, **8**:*39*
and the Sand Creek Massacre **1**:41, **8**:60
Arawak **2**:10, **3**:18–19, **4**:15
Arctic and Subarctic tribal groups 1:*20*, **43–5**
canoes **2**:47
clothing **3**:12–13
hunting **1**:43, **4**:*20*, *60*
see also igloos
Argall, Samuel **3**:56
Arikara **2**:41, **4**:*37*, 53, **8**:*55*, **10**:*28*, 29–*30*, 31, 42
art 1:46–8
see also under various arts and crafts
assimilation **3**:63–4, **8**:12–13
Assiniboine 1:49–50, **3**:34–5, 38, **4**:56
Astor, Jacob **4**:32
astronomy *see* cosmology
Athapascan 1:51–3, **2**:9
Athapascan speakers 1:45, **54–5**, **2**:8 *see also* Hupa
atlatls **4**:59
Aztec Ruins **5**:41
Aztecs 1:56–9, **4**:*10*, **5**:*50*, **6**:52, **8**:54
and the afterlife **1**:11
and Casa Grande **2**:51
corn **4**:*28*
fasting and bloodletting **4**:10
human sacrifice **1**:57–8, **3**:51, **8**:*45*, **9**:55
language **10**:34
rituals **2**:11–12, **8**:*45*
and the Spanish conquest **1**:*57*, 58–9, **3**:28–9, 33, **9**:41
and the Toltec **10**:6
see also Tenochtitlán
Aztec-Tanoan **9**:50, **10**:34
Azul, Antonio **7**:47

B

babies **2**:*11*, 24
see also birth customs; children
Bad Axe, Battle of **2**:*18*, *23*
balsas **2**:48
bands **1**:38, **3**:20, **4**:38, 59, 63, **7**:4, 49
Baranov, Aleksandr **8**:51
Barboncito (Navajo chief) **7**:10, 11
bark
see birchbark; elm bark
Bascom Affair (1861) **3**:16
Basin and Plateau 1:60–2, **4**:49
see also Klamath; Modoc; Nez Percé; Paiute; Salish; Ute
Basket-Maker Culture **1**:34
basketry 1:34, **63–4**, **4**:*22*, 58
Apache **1**:38
Klamath **5**:*43*
Modoc **6**:*42*, 44
Nez Percé **1**:*62*, 63, **3**:24
Nootka **7**:*20*
Paiute **7**:37, *38*
Papago and Pima **7**:*45*, 46, *47*
Pomo **1**:*63*, **7**:60
Winnebago **1** *46*
Bat Cave 1:12, **2:4**
beads **5**:25, 27, **8**:28–9, **10**:*13*, 14
see also quillwork and beadwork
beans **1**:12, 14
bears **1**:*54*, **4**:*59*, **9**:*25*, 49, **10**:*9*, *11*
bear-claw necklaces **10**:42
Beaver Men **2**:33
Beaver Wars **5**:35
Beecher Island, Battle of **5**:10–11
Bella Coola, masks **6**:*12*
Bent, George **3**:*60*
Benteen, Frederick **5**:*59*
Beothuk 2:5, **4**:9
berdaches **2**:14
Bering, Vitus **8**:50
Bering Bridge 1:43, 51, **2:6–7**, **4**:52, **5**:14
Big Bear (chief) **3**:41, **8**:43
Big Foot (Sioux chief) **5**:*10*, 12, **10**:*59*, 60
Big Time **7**:60
birchbark 1:*51*, **2:8–9**, 47, **3**:38, **6**:*32*, **7**:5, 25
see also canoes
birth customs 2:10–12, 62, **9**:48
bison *see* buffalo
Black Bear (Arapaho chief) **8**:*37*
black drink **9**:*34*
Black Elk 2:13, **9**:45–6
Blackfoot 1:24, **2:14–17**, *24*, **3**:*35*, **6**:*22*, **10**:*7*
beadwork **8**:29
Beaver Men **2**:33
sacred sites **2**:*15*, **8**:*54*
and travois **2**:15, **7**:*55*
tribal conflicts **1**:50, **2**:15, 17, **9**:*28*
warrior societies **2**:14–15, **10**:48
see also Crowfoot (chief)
Blackfoot Treaty (1877) **3**:*47*
Black Hawk (Sauk and Fox chief) **2**:18, *23*, **6**:20, **8**:64
Black Hawk's War **2**:18, **8**:64
Black Hills **2**:19–20, 56, **3**:36, *37*, **5**:11–12, 48, 58, **8**:36, **9**:30, 31, **10**:59
Black Kettle (Cheyenne chief) **5**:10, 11, **8**:*60*
Black Mesa **4**:50
blankets *see* rugs and blankets
bloodletting **4**:10, 11
Bodmer, Karl **10**:29, 30–1, *46*
body adornment 2:21–4
see also feathers; jewelry; tattoos
Bonampak 2:25–6
Boone, Daniel **1**:33

Bosque Redondo 2:27, 50, 7:11
Bowlegs, Billy (Seminole chief) 9:10
bows and arrows 2:28–9
Bozeman Trail 5:11, 8:36, 37, 9:29, 30
Braddock, Edward 7:26, 61
Brant, Joseph (Mohawk chief) 1:32–3, 2:30–1, 4:30, 6:49
breastplates 8:51, 10:42
British colonization, and Native Americans 5:31, 33–4, 47, 6:64
British Northwest Company 6:28
Brulé Sioux 8:37
buffalo 1:14, 2:14, 19, 32–4, 5:38, 7:55, 57, 9:27
  and the cattle trails 2:52, 53
  dying out 2:34, 53, 3:44, 5:38, 7:57, 8:31–2, 10:59
  extinct bison 2:6–7, 32, 4:25
  and the horse 1:62, 4:53–4, 60
  and the railroads 2:34, 8:31–2
  and rituals/ceremonies 2:33, 34, 6:22, 23, 8:46, 10:31
Buffalo Bill's Wild West Show 2:13, 9:31, 32
bullboats 2:48
Bureau of Indian Affairs (BIA) 2:35–7, 3:64, 5:53, 54, 6:45, 10:21, 60
  occupation of (1972) 2:37, 6:17, 7:44, 10:22
Burgoa, Friar 6:41
burial bowls 6:47, 48
burial grounds 9:48
burial mounds
  Adena-Hopewell 1:7, 8
  at Cahokia 2:43
  at Mound Spiro 6:55
  Mound City 6:53–4
burials 1:10, 2:43, 3:52, 53, 54
  at Jaina 5:24
  at Monte Alban 6:52
  at Palenque 7:40
  Olmec 5:51
  and totem poles 10:10
  see also ceremonies, burial; death, customs
Bushy Run, Battle of 7:64
Busk *see* Green Corn ceremony
Butterfield Overland Mail route 6:4

C

cacti 7:45
  peyote 7:54
Caddo 2:38–40, 41
Caddoan speakers 2:41–2, 7:49
Cahokia (city) 2:42–3, 4:8, 6:39, 7:62, 8:25, 26, 54–5, 9:35
Cahokia (tribe) 2:42
calendars
  Aztec 1:57, 3:33
  Mayan 1:57, 3:6, 31, 32–3, 6:16
  Olmec 7:28
Californian tribal groups 2:44–6, 3:12, 4:27, 58
  balsas 2:48
  featherwork 4:15
  and fish 4:19
  gambling 4:33
  jewelry 2:45, 5:25
  see also Chumash; Hupa; mission Indians; Pomo
calumets 9:28–9, 64
Calusa 6:64, 9:59
Canada Firsters 8:38
Canadian Mounted Police (Mounties) 1:17, 3:41, 47
Canby, Edward 6:46
candlefish 4:28
canoes 2:47–8, 5:20, 42, 45
  birchbark 1:19, 2:5, 9, 47, 7:24
  dugout 2:47, 48, 4:44, 5:42, 7:22, 9:8
  with sails 5:44
  seal 4:19
  see also kayaks
Canyon de Chelly 2:27, 49–50, 4:49, 7:31, 8:17
Caonabo (chief) 3:19
Captain Jack (Kintpuash) 6:45–6
Cardenas, Garcia Lopez de 3:27
caribou 7:5
Carleton, James C. 2:27
Carson, Kit 2:27, 50, 7:10–11
Cartier, Jacques 4:31, 10:12
Casa Grande 2:51, 7:45
Casas, Bartolomé de las 2:60
casinos 4:34, 5:54
Catawba 5:32, 7:8
Catholicism
  Sonoran 7:46
  see also missionaries; missions
Catlin, George 2:28, 7:24, 9:24, 10:29
  paintings by 1:49, 3:20, 22, 49, 4:52, 8:44, 9:29, 10:31
cattle, raising 2:53
cattle trails 2:52–3
caves, sacred 8:54
Cayuga 1:32, 2:31
Cayuse 1:62, 4:53
cedar 9:62
ceremonies 6:19
  adulthood 3:61–2
  agricultural 3:25, 4:22–3, 8:45
  at medicine wheels 6:23
  banned 3:44
  bark rolls used in 2:9
  birth 2:10–11, 62
  burial 1:10, 2:43
  human sacrifice 1:57–8, 8:45
  kachina 5:29–30, 40, 8:20
  Midewiwin 6:31, 32
  naming 2:10–11, 12, 62, 9:46
  puberty 1:40, 8:46
  renewal 2:33, 57, 10:30
  sand painting 8:62
  sings 7:12
  sweat lodge 9:45, 46
  tobacco 3:44
  totem-pole raising 10:23, 24
  Turkey Dance 2:39
  and wampums 10:40
  see also Ghost Dance; potlatches; rituals
Chac (rain god) 6:15–16, 10:35
Chac, Lord 10:35
Chaco Canyon 2:54–5
  see also Pueblo Bonito
Champlain, Samuel de 1:18, 10:12
Chandalar Kutchin 1:52
Charbonneau, Toussaint 8:52–3
Charles II, King 4:55
charms 1:54, 10:42
Cherokee 1:28, 3:52, 4:21–4, 30, 7:8
  relocation 4:23, 9:36, 10:15, 16, 20–1
  and the Revolutionary War 1:32, 4:23
  taboos 9:49
  villages 10:57–8
  written language 9:13
  see also Trail of Tears
Cheyenne 1:42, 2:53, 56–9, 3:21–2, 7:54
  Battle of Little Bighorn 2:59
  death customs 3:54
  Hoof-Rattle Society 2:33
  marriage 6:6
  reservations 1:41, 42, 2:59
  taboos 9:47–8
  warriors 2:57, 58, 10:49
  see also Indian Wars; Sand Creek Massacre
Chiapas 2:60
  cities *see* Bonampak; Palenque
Chichén Itzá *see* Chitchén Itzá
Chichimec 10:6, 27
Chickasaw 2:53, 4:21, 6:62, 7:8
  and the Civil War 1:28
  and Queen Anne's War 8:27
  relocation 4:23, 10:16, 21
chickees 4:48–9, 9:7, 35
Chief Mountain 2:15, 8:54
children 2:61–4, 3:43
  as apprentice warriors 10:45–6
  named 2:10–11, 12, 62, 9:46
  reincarnation 1:9
  sacrificed 7:7
  see also education; games; puberty; Vision Quest
Chilkat, blankets 8:48, 9:62, 10:24
Chinook 3:4–5, 8:59
Chinook Jargon 3:5, 5:42
Chippewa *see* Ojibway
Chiricahua Apache 1:36
  see also Cochise (chief); Geronimo (chief)
Chisholm, Jesse 2:52
Chisholm Trail 2:52, 53
Chitchén Itzá 3:6, 10:5–6, 35
Chivington, J. M. 2:57, 58, 5:10, 8:60
Choctaw 2:53, 4:21, 23, 6:62–3, 64
  and the Caddo 2:40
  and the Civil War 1:28
  and the Natchez 7:8
  and Queen Anne's War 8:27
  relocation 4:23, 10:16, 21
Christianity *see* religion
Chumash 2:45, 46, 48, 3:7, 6:36
Church, Benjamin 5:34
Cibola *see* Seven Cities of Cibola/gold
cities *see* urban life
citizenship, U.S. 5:4, 53, 7:42
  and the Allotment Act 1:26
clans 3:8–9, 4:63, 10:9, 63
Clark, George Rogers 1:33, 9:23
cliff dwellings 1:15, 34, 35, 3:10, 6:24, 8:17
  see also Mesa Verde
Cliff Palace 1:34, 3:10, 6:25
clothing 3:11–14, 4:24
  Apache 1:39, 40, 3:17
  and beadwork 8:29
  Ghost Dance 4:42
  Inuit 3:12–13, 5:15
  marriage 3:4
  Naskapi 7:5
  Osage 7:32
  see also headdresses; jewelry; moccasins; war costumes
Clovis 2:7, 4:25
clowns, kachina 5:29, 30, 8:20
clubs (weapons) 4:63, 7:25, 10:7, 46
Coast Salish 3:14, 15, 51, 8:48, 59
Cochise (chief) 1:37, 2:4, 3:16–17, 4:39, 6:4
  movies depicting 6:58
Cochise culture 2:4, 8:47
Code Talkers, Navajo 7:11
Cody, Buffalo Bill 6:57
Collier, John 2:36
Colorado Volunteers 5:10
Columbus, Christopher 3:18–19, 24, 4:27, 6:33, 9:16
Comanche 1:36, 42, 2:53, 3:20–2, 9:50
  beadwork 8:29
  drums 6:60
  Kiowa allies 3:21, 5:37, 39
  language 10:34
  marriage 6:7, 8
  and peyote 7:54
Company of New France 10:12
compass bearings 3:32
concho belts 7:11
confederacies 4:8
Constitution, U.S. 5:23, 10:22
Contraires 2:57
cooking 1:63, 4:28, 9:52
Copán 3:23, 31
copper 5:26–7, 8:7
corn 1:14, 3:24–5, 4:22–3, 26, 28, 9:14
  in Bat Cave 1:12, 2:4
  first farmed 1:12, 6:13–14
Cornstalk (Shawnee chief) 1:33, 9:23
Coronado, Francisco de 1:5, 2:27, 41, 3:26–7, 29, 4:50, 7:50, 8:18, 23, 9:41, 10:62
Corte Real, Caspar 2:5
Cortés, Hernando 1:58, 59, 3:28–9, 6:26, 9:40–1, 56, 10:5
cosmology 3:7, 30–3, 4:4, 9:46
  Aztec 8:45
  and the Caddoan peoples 2:41
  and Cahokia 2:43
  and medicine wheels 6:23, 8:55–6
cotton 1:14, 3:11
Council Springs Treaty 2:40
coup, counting 1:39, 2:15, 3:34–5, 4:13, 5:39, 10:46, 49

Court of Claims **5**:4, 5
Cowichan **8**:48
Coyolxauhqui **1**:57
crafts *see* art
Crazy Horse (Sioux chief)
  2:20, **3**:**36–7**, **5**:12, 59, 60, 61, **8**:36, **9**:30
creation *see* origin myths
Cree **3**:**38–41**, 60, **4**:56, **9**:49
  and bark **2**:8–9, **3**:38
  crafts **8**:28
  iron traps **10**:14
  mixed-race *see* Métis
  names **2**:12
  and the Riel Rebellions **8**:43
  and scalping **9**:28
  travois **10**:*17*
Creek **4**:*21*, *22*, 24, **6**:*62*, 63–4, **7**:8, **9**:60
  and the Civil War **1**:28, *29*
  death customs **3**:52
  relocation **4**:*23*, **10**:21
  and the War of 1812 **10**:44
Creek War **7**:35
Crook, George **3**:17, **9**:5
  and Geronimo **4**:39, *40*
  and the Sioux **3**:36, 37, **5**:12, 59, 61
crops *see* agriculture
Crow **1**:10, **2**:53, *62*, **3**:**42–5**, **4**:*17*, **6**:*18*, 23
  beadwork **8**:29
  clothing **3**:*11*, *13*, *42*
  counting coup **3**:34, 35
  hair **2**:23, **3**:42–3
  medicine bundles **6**:*20*, *21*
  and the Nez Percé **7**:18
  scouts **9**:5
  tobacco **9**:63
  warrior societies **10**:48
Crow Dog **3**:**46**
Crowfoot (Blackfoot chief)
  2:17, **3**:**47**
cults, secret religious
  10:63–4
Custer, George A. **2**:*20*, 59, **3**:36, 44, **5**:11–12, *58*, 59–*60*, **9**:30, *32*, **10**:*37*, 60
  movies depicting **6**:58
  scouts **9**:5

D
Dade Massacre **9**:12
Dakota (Santee) Sioux
  4:12–13, **7**:26, **9**:26, 27
  Little Crow **5**:62
Dale, Thomas **7**:58, 59
dams **10**:*51*
dance **3**:35, **48–51**
  animals represented **4**:26
  Apache **1**:*38*
  Coast Salish **3**:15
  Ghost Dance **1**:42, **4**:42
  Hopi **1**:*13*, **3**:*48*, 49–50, **4**:*14*
  hunting **3**:50–1, **10**:31
  kachina **3**:*48*, **5**:29, 30, **8**:20, 45
  matachina **6**:61
  rain **3**:50, **4**:4, 14, **10**:*62*
  Seminole **9**:*8*
  war **9**:*37*, *61*
Danger Cave **4**:*58*
Davis, Edwin H. **6**:54
Dawes Act *see* Allotment Act (1887)
Day and Night Dance **8**:*44*
death
  customs **1**:*10*, **3**:43, **52–5**, **5**:24, **6**:*11*, **7**:7
  and reincarnation **1**:9
  taboos **9**:*48*
  see also afterlife; burials
Deerfield Massacre **8**:*27*
dehorning **10**:52
Dekanawaidah/Deganawida
  4:45, **5**:22
Delaware **1**:33, **3**:**56–8**, **5**:31–2, **7**:63, 64, **9**:22, **10**:*40*
Delaware Prophet **7**:63
Detroit, Siege of (1763) **7**:26, 62
Diegueno **2**:45, **6**:*33*
Discovery, HMS **5**:*45*
diseases *see* epidemics
disenfranchisement **3**:**59–60**
divorce **6**:8
Dog Soldiers **2**:57, **10**:49
dolls **2**:*63*, **8**:11, **9**:*10*
  kachina **4**:14, *51*, **5**:*29*, 30, **8**:20
Dramatizations of Dreams **3**:15
dreams and visions **2**:46, **3**:57, **5**:39, **6**:21, **10**:47
  shaman **9**:21
  and sweat lodges **9**:45,
  see also Vision Quest
droughts **1**:13, 15, **2**:51
drums/drumming **1**:*50*, **3**:48, **6**:*60*, **10**:*23*, *24*
Dull Knife (Cheyenne chief)
  8:37
Duncan, William **10**:26
Dustin, Hannah **5**:36

E
Eagle Dance **4**:*14*
eagles **3**:*44*, **4**:*12*, *14*, 15, **6**:*18*, **10**:*64*
ears, pierced **2**:10, 12, *23*, 24, 62
Ecuyer, Simeon **4**:6
education **2**:*36*, **3**:**61–4**, **5**:*39*, 54
  and alcohol abuse **1**:17
  elderly, the **3**:54, **9**:28
Elle of Ganado **10**:*54*
elm bark **2**:8, *9*, 47, **4**:48, 49, **8**:*63*, **10**:*57*
El Tajín **3**:*32*, **4**:4, **8**:26
encomienda system **2**:60
Endecott, John **7**:53
epidemics **1**:41, 59, **4**:**5–6**, 9, 44, **5**:45, **9**:40
  smallpox **1**:49, **2**:17, **4**:*5*, 6, 9, 63, **5**:45, **7**:57, 64, **9**:41
Erdrich, Louise **4**:7, **5**:56, **7**:26
Eric the Red **5**:17
Escalante, Francisco Silvestre
  6:24
Eskimos **5**:14
  see also Inuit
Espéjo, Antonio de **1**:5
eulachon **4**:28, **10**:24
Evans, John **2**:59, **8**:60
extinction **4**:**8–9**

F
facepaint **2**:*21*, *24*, **3**:49–50
Fallen Timbers, Battle of
  3:*58*, **9**:23, 53
families, and totem poles
  10:9, 10–11
farming *see* agriculture
fasting **4**:**10–11**
Feast of the Dead **1**:10
feathers
  featherwork **4**:**14–15**, 58
  for warriors **3**:*17*, **4**:**12–13**, **9**:*24*, **10**:42
federal aid **8**:*14*, 34–5
Fernandeno people **6**:35
festivals **1**:*5*, **7**:13, **10**:64
  agricultural **4**:22–3, **8**:45
  see also ceremonies
Fetterman Massacre **5**:11, *12*
Fetterman, William **5**:11
firearms **2**:*14*, **4**:**16–17**, 60, **10**:13–14
  and shields **9**:25
Firsters **8**:38
fishing **4**:**18–19**, 27–8, **10**:24
  rights **4**:**20**
  salmon **3**:4, *5*, 50, **4**:18–19, 60, **5**:44, **7**:20, **8**:**59**, **9**:62, **10**:*51*
Five Civilized Tribes
  4:**21–4**, **6**:64, **9**:36
  and the Civil War **1**:28, 29, 30, **4**:24
  and the Indian Territory
  4:*23*, 24, **5**:8, **9**:9, **10**:16
  see also Cherokee; Chickasaw; Choctaw; Creek; Seminole; Trail of Tears
Five Nations *see* Iroquois
flags **3**:*33*
Flathead Salish **8**:*57*, *58*
flint tips **4**:*25*
Florida
  and Hernando de Soto
  9:33, 59–60
  Jackson's invasion of **9**:11
  missions **6**:37
  see also Southeast/Florida tribes
Folsom and Clovis **2**:6–7, **4**:25
food **4**:**26–8**
  and Californian tribes **2**:44
  cattle as **2**:53
  see also agriculture; cooking; fishing; gathering; hunting
Fort Dearborn **10**:*43*, 44
Fort Duquesne **4**:29, 30
Fort Garry **8**:*38*
Fort Laramie **4**:*32*
Fort Laramie Treaty (1851)
  2:58, **3**:45, **9**:29
Fort Laramie Treaty (1868)
  2:20, **3**:36, 45, **5**:*4*, 11, 58, **8**:36, 37, **9**:31, **10**:*22*
Fort Meigs **9**:*54*
Fort Peck Indian Agency **1**:50
Fort Phil Kearney **8**:36, *37*
Fort Saint Frédéric **5**:32
Fort Saratoga **5**:32
Fort Wayne Treaty (1809) **1**:17
Forty Years of Famine **7**:47
Fox *see* Sauk and Fox
Fray Marcos **3**:26
Fremont, John Charles **6**:44
French colonists, and Native Americans **5**:31, **7**:7–8
French and Indian War
  1:20, 23–4, **4**:**29–30**, 31, 56, **7**:61, **10**:13
French missions **4**:56, **6**:37
Frobisher, Martin **5**:17
Frontenac, Comte de **5**:35
funerals *see* burials
furs, as clothing **3**:12, 14
fur trade **4**:**31–2**, **8**:50–1, **10**:26
  and the Algonquian **1**:19
  and Algonquian speakers
  1:23
  and the Chinook **3**:4–5
  and the Cree **3**:39–40, 41, **6**:27–8
  and the Huron **4**:64
  and the Ojibway **1**:23, **4**:56, **7**:26
  see also Hudson's Bay Company

G
Gadsden Purchase (1853) **7**:46
Gaines, Edmund **9**:8
Gall (chief) **3**:36
gambling **4**:**33–4**
games **4**:4, 22, **35–6**, **7**:21
  see also lacrosse
gans (mountain spirits) **1**:40
gathering **4**:27, **37–8**
  see also hunter-gatherers
General Allotment Act
  see Allotment Act (1887)
genocide, colonial **2**:5
George, Chief Dan **6**:*58*
George II, king of Britain
  5:31, *32*
Geronimo (Apache chief)
  1:*26*, 37, *39*, **4**:**39–40**, **6**:20
Ghost Dance **1**:*42*, **3**:46, **4**:**41–2**, **6**:38, **7**:54, **9**:30, **10**:59, 60
  and Wounded Knee
  7:38, **10**:60
  and Wovoka **1**:61, **4**:41–2, **7**:38, **9**:32, **10**:59, 61
gods
  Apache **1**:*40*, **9**:*39*
  Aztec **1**:57, *59*, **3**:6, **4**:*28*
  Mayan **6**:*15*–16, **7**:*30*
  Olmec **7**:28
  Papago and Pima **7**:46
  Sioux **9**:28
gold
  Californian Gold Rush **5**:8, **6**:36, **7**:47, 60
  gold prospectors **1**:50, *53*, 62, **4**:61, **5**:10, **7**:38
  and Hernando de Soto **9**:33
  in the Black Hills **2**:19–20, **5**:11–12, 58
  and the Modoc **6**:44
  and Nez Percé territory **7**:15
  see also Bozeman Trail; Oregon Trail
Goodnight-Loving Trail **2**:52, *53*
Gosuite **1**:61
government, federal, support from **5**:54
government, tribal **2**:56–7, **5**:23, 52, 53–4, **6**:29–30
Grand Alliance, War of the
  5:35
Grand Medicine Lodge **2**:9
grandparents **2**:*62*, 63, **3**:62
grasshoppers, hunting **1**:61
Great Depression **2**:36

Great Lakes region **7**:24
wild rice **4**:*27*, 58, **7**:25
see also Ojibway; Tecumseh
Great Law of Peace **5**:22–3
Great Medicine/Mystery/Spirit **3**:33, *37*, **6**:19, 31, **9**:28, 45
Great Medicine Society
see Midewiwin
Great Plains *see* Plains tribes
Great Serpent Mound
see Serpent Mound
Great Spirit
see Great Medicine/Mystery/Spirit
Great Sun **2**:42, **7**:6, 7
Great World Tree **3**:32
Green Corn ceremony **3**:25, **4**:22–3, **9**:36
Groseilliers, Médard de **4**:55
Gros Ventre **1**:41
Guacata **6**:64
Guadalupe Hidalgo, Treaty of (1848) **7**:10
guns *see* firearms

H

Haida 4:43–4, **8**:59
masks **1**:*9*, 10, **4**:*44*, **6**:11
hair **2**:*23*, **3**:42–3, 57, **6**:*7*, **7**:*49*
hair pipes **10**:42
Hamilton, Henry **1**:33
Hamtsa Dance **3**:50, **6**:10
hand game **4**:*33–4*
Handsome Lake (Iroquois chief) **5**:63
Harrison, William H. **1**:17, **9**:54, **10**:43
hats **7**:*20*, *38*, **8**:*6*, *7*
headbands **2**:24
headdresses **7**:*21*
ritual/ceremonial **9**:*20*, *47*, *62*, **10**:*25*
warrior **7**:*34*, **10**:42, *48*
see also hats; war costumes
head flattening **2**:23–4
heads, stone **5**:*50*, **7**:*27*, 28–9
Hiawatha 4:45, **5**:22, 57
Hidatsa **3**:43, **4**:13, **9**:26, **10**:29, *30*, 31, *49*
hide **2**:*33*, **8**:47
highways, Anasazi **2**:55
Hispaniola **2**:10, **3**:19, 28, *54*
Hitchiti **6**:63
Hogan, Linda **5**:*55*
hogans **4**:*49*, **7**:12, **8**:62
Hohokam 1:15, 25, 34, **2**:4, **3**:25, **4**:**46**, **7**:45, **8**:10, **9**:64
Holt, Gustav **5**:*16*
homes 4:47–9
adobe **1**:15, 34, **2**:54, **6**:14
Apache **1**:38–9 48, **8**:21
Arctic **1**:44, **4**:*47*, **5**:14, *17*
at Canyon de Chelly **2**:*49*–50, **4**:*49*, **8**:*17*
at Chaco Canyon **2**:*54–5*, **8**:22
Athapascan **1**:51
Aztec (at Tenochtitlán) **9**:55
and bark **2**:8
Caddo **2**:39
chickees **4**:48–9, **9**:7, 35
Choctaw **6**:*64*
cliff dwellings **1**:15, *34*, *35*, **3**:10, **6**:24–5, **8**:*17*
earth-lodges **4**:48, **6**:42–3, **7**:49, *51*, **10**:29
high-rise/multistory **1**:15, **2**:54, *55*, **4**:49, **6**:24–5, **8**:19, 22
hogans **4**:*49*, **7**:12
Klamath **5**:*42*
lodges **7**:*4*, **8**:*63*
longhouses **1**:22, **4**:44, *63*, **5**:20, *22–3*, **7**:21
multifamily **4**:44, 48, **10**:24–5
of the Adena **1**:7
Ojibway **7**:*26*
Olmec **7**:27–8
pit-houses **1**:34, **2**:4, 54, **6**:47, 48
plank **4**:48, *61*, **7**:21, 22
wickiups **1**:39, **2**:*44*, **4**:49, **7**:36, *60*
see also pueblos; tepees; wigwams
Homestead Act (1862) **9**:18
Hoof-Rattle Society **2**:33
Hooker Jim **6**:*45*
Hopewell and Adena 1:7–8, **5**:*26*
see also Mound City
Hopi 1:6, **2**:50, **4**:*9*, **50–1**, **8**:24, 30
agricultural ceremonies **8**:45
crafts **4**:*14*, **8**:*9*, 47, 48
dance **1**:*13*, **3**:*48*, 49–50, **4**:*14*, 51, **6**:10, 11
flute ceremony **6**:*60*
homes **4**:49
language **10**:34
and marriage **6**:*7*
reincarnation **1**:9
songs for rain **6**:60
see also kachinas
hops **1**:*15*
horses 1:62, **4**:**52–4**, **8**:24, **10**:14
introduced by the Spanish **1**:36–7, **4**:52–3, **9**:40
and the Nez Percé **1**:62, **7**:14
painted **10**:42
Plains **2**:15–16, 56; **3**:20–1, *22*, **4**:*53*, 60, **5**:39, **7**:50, **8**:24
raiding **3**:20–1, 44, **4**:54, **5**:39
travois **7**:*55*, **10**:*17*, *18*
Horseshoe Bend, Battle of **10**:44
Huastec **4**:4, **6**:13
Hudson's Bay Company **1**:*16*, **2**:17, **3**:5, 41, **4**:31, 55–6, **6**:27, **8**:38, **10**:12, 26
Huitzilopochtli **1**:57, 59
hunter-gatherers 1:12, **4**:37, **57–8**, 60, **6**:33–4
Klamath **5**:42–3
Micmac **6**:29
see also gathering
hunting 4:27–8, **59–60**
and the Algonquian **1**:18–19
in the Arctic/Subarctic **1**:43–4, **4**:*20*, *60*
by Paleo-Indians **4**:25
dances **3**:50–1, **10**:31
eagles **4**:15
grasshoppers **1**:61
taboos **9**:49
see also buffalo; fishing; rituals
Hupa 1:54, **2**:46, **4**:15, **61**
Huron 4:62–4, **6**:49, **8**:28, **10**:57, *58*
and birchbark **2**:*8*
birth ceremonies **2**:10

I

igloos **1**:44, **4**:*47*, **5**:14, *17*
IITC (International Indian Treaty Council) **7**:44
Indian Claims Commission 5:4–5, **7**:38
Indian Claims Limitation Act (1982) **5**:49
Indian New Deal **2**:37
Indian Religion Freedom Act (1934) **9**:21
Indian Religious Freedom Act (1978) **7**:54
Indian Removal Act (1830) **3**:60, **4**:24, **5**:7–8, 9, **7**:35, **9**:8–9, 18, 36, **10**:15
see also Trail of Tears
Indian Reorganization Act (1934) **1**:26, **9**:10
Indian Self-Determination and Education Assistance Act (1975) **7**:51
Indian Shaker Church **6**:38
Indian Status **5**:52, **8**:5
Indian Territory 1:42, **3**:60, **4**:*23*, 24, **5**:**6–8**, **8**:40–1
and the Civil War **1**:*27–30*
dissolved **1**:42, **4**:24, **7**:34, 51
and the Osage **7**:33–4
see also Trail of Tears
Indian Wars 5:9–12, **8**:32, **10**:18
see also Little Bighorn, Battle of; Sand Creek Massacre; Wounded Knee
Institute of American Indian Arts **1**:48
integration *see* assimilation
International Indian Treaty Council (IITC) **7**:44
interpreters 5:**13**
Inuit 1:43, *44*, **5**:**14–17**, **6**:30
birth ceremonies **2**:10–11
body adornment **2**:23, **5**:15–16
clothing **3**:*12*–13, **5**:15
dance **3**:50
homes **4**:*47*, **5**:14, *17*
hunting/fishing **4**:*20*, *60*, **5**:15
kayaks **2**:47, **5**:*14*, 16
masks **6**:*12*
Olympics **4**:*36*
and the Russians **8**:51
taboos **9**:47
Inuit speakers 5:**18**
Inupiaq language **5**:18
Ipai **6**:34, 35
Iroquoian speakers 5:**19**, **10**:57
Iroquois 4:9, **5**:**20–3**, *53*
and bark **2**:8, **5**:20
birth ceremonies **2**:10
crafts **5**:*21*, **8**:28, 29
dance **3**:51, **5**:*64*, **6**:10
death customs **1**:10
farming **1**:14, **5**:20
and the French and Indian War **4**:*29*, 30
and guns **4**:17, **5**:23
homes **4**:48, **5**:20
and King William's War **5**:35, 36
League of Nations **1**:32, **4**:45, **5**:20,**10**:40
masks **3**:24, *25*, **6**:10, 11, 12
Midwinter Festival **8**:45
origin myths **7**:30
rattles **6**:60–1
religion **5**:21–2, 63–4, **6**:19
and the Revolutionary War **1**:*32–3*, **2**:30–1
sacred societies **5**:63, 64, **6**:22
shell-money **5**:26
totems **10**:9
tribal conflicts **1**:21–2, *23*, **4**:62, 64, **7**:26
wampums **10**:40
women **10**:52
see also Brant, Joseph; Cayuga; Mohawk; Oneida; Onondaga; Seneca; Tuscarora
irrigation **2**:51, **3**:25, **4**:46, **7**:27, 45
Isleta **8**:17
Itzcoatl **10**:6

J

Jackson, Andrew
as general **9**:8, 11, 36, **10**:44
relocation policies **4**:24, **7**:35, **9**:9, 36, **10**:15, *16*
jade **6**:*11*, 15, **7**:*29*
Jaina 5:**24**
James Bay Project **3**:60
Jamestown **8**:15, *16*, **9**:16, 17
Jenkin's Ear, War of **5**:31
jewelry 2:24, *45*, **4**:19, *61*, **5**:**25–7**, **7**:*9*, **10**:*63*
medicine necklaces **6**:*19*
turquoise **8**:*19*, *22*
Jicarilla **1**:36, **3**:9, *33*, **4**:49
Johnson, William **2**:30, **5**:23, 32
Joseph, Chief 5:**28**, 56, **7**:*13*, 15, 16, 17, 18
Juh **4**:39
Jumping Dance **4**:15

K

kachinas 1:9, **3**:25, *52*, **4**:51, **5**:**29–30**, 40, **6**:19, **8**:18, **9**:38, **10**:63
clowns **5**:29, 30, **8**:20
dances **3**:*48*, **5**:29, 30, **6**:10, **8**:20, 45
dolls **4**:14, *51*, **5**:*29*, 30, **8**:20, **9**:38
kivas of **5**:41
masks **4**:14, **6**:10, 11, 12, **8**:20, **9**:38
Kadohadacho tribes *see* Caddo
Kaigani **4**:*43*
Kansas, white settlers **5**:*6*, *7*, 8
Karok **2**:46
kayaks **2** 47, **5**:*14*, 16
Keokuk (Sauk chief) **2**:18, **8**:*64*
kettles **5**:27
Keuuyit **7**:13
Kicking Bird (Kiowa chief) **5**:*39*

King George's War 5:31–2
King Hendrick (Mohawk chief) 5:*19*
King Philip's War 5:33–4
King William's War 5:35–6
Kino, Eusebio Francisco 2:51
Kintpuash (Captain Jack) 6:*45–6*
Kiowa 1:42, 2:53, 3:21–2, **5:37–9**, 7:54, 9:50
marriage 6:*6*
warriors 5:39, 10:49
Kiowa-Apache 1:36, 5:37
Kishkekosh 8:*63*
kivas 1:34, 2:49, 3:*10*, 4:46, 5:29–30, **40–1**, 9:46
at Chaco Canyon 2:*54*, 55, 8:*21*, 22
and clans 3:9
and masks 6:12
Klamath 1:62, **5:42–3**, 6:42, 45
knitting 3:*14*, 15
knives 10:*12*
Konieschquanoheel 3:57
Kutchin 1:*45*
Kutenai 2:17
Kwakiutl 3:*8*, 50–1, **5:44–5**, 6:*10*, 60, 10:*14*

L

lacrosse 4:22, *35*, 36, 5:**46**, 7:63–4
Laguna 8:17
Lakota (Teton) Sioux 3:*49*, 9:26, 27
death customs 3:54
and the Ghost Dance 7:38, 9:32, 10:59
Sun Dance lodges 3:32
see also Black Elk; Ghost Dance; Red Cloud; Sitting Bull; Wounded Knee
Land Offices 5:7
land rights 3:60, **5:47–9**
and the Allotment Act 1:25–6, 3:60
and the Black Hills 2:20
and the Bureau of Indian Affairs 2:35
and the Indian Claims Commission 5:4–5
and the Indian Reorganization Act 1:26
land surrendered 3:*59*, 60
and William Penn 3:*57*
see also treaties
land rushes 5:*5*, *6*
landscapes 5:47–*8*, 8:54–5, *56*
language
Chinook Jargon 3:5, 5:42
Eskimo-Aleut 5:18
interpreters 5:13
Iroquois 5:19
Muskogean 6:62
Siouan 9:26
Tanoan 9:50, 10:34
Uto-Aztecan 9:50, 10:34
see also Sequoyah
Last of the Mohicans, The (novel and film) 6:50, 57
La Venta 5:50–1, 7:*29*
Lawyer (Nez Percé chief) 7:15
League of Augsburg, War of 5:*35*
legends/stories 1:53, 5:55, *56*, 6:10, 8:6, 10:54
legislation 5:52–4
see also recognition
Le Jeune, Paul 7:4–5
Lenni Lenape *see* Delaware
Lewis and Clark expedition 7:14, *15*, *33*, 8:*52–3*, 10:28–9
license plates 5:*38*
Lillooet 8:58
Lipan 1:36
lip rings 2:23
literature 5:55–7, 10:55
Louise Erdrich **4:7**, 5:56
see also Sequoyah
Little Bighorn, Battle of 2:13, *20*, 59, 3:35, 36, 44–5, 5:12, **58–61**, 9:30, *32*
and scouts 9:5
Little Crow 5:62
Little Raven (Southern Arapaho chief) 1:42
Livermore, Earl 7:*42*
lodges 7:*4*, 8:*63*
earth-lodges 4:48, 6:42–3, 7:49, *51*, 10:29
Sun-Dance 3:32
see also sweat lodges
Lone Wolf (Kiowa chief) 5:38, 39
Longfellow, Henry 4:*45*
longhouse religion 5:63–4
longhouses 1:22, 4:44, *63*, 5:20, *22–3*, *64*, 7:21
Long Walk 7:11
Lords of Xibalba 1:11
Louisbourg 5:*31*, 32
Louisiana Purchase 7:26, 50
Lumbee 8:*35*
Lyon, Nathaniel 1:*29*

M

Mabila, Battle of 9:33
Macdonald, John 8:43
McDougall, William 8:38
McGillivray, Alexander 6:64
McIntosh, Chief 4:*21*
McJunkin, George 4:25
Mahican 6:50
Mahsette-Kuiuab (chief) 3:*41*
Major Crimes Act (1885) 5:53–4
Malecite 6:30
Malinche 6:26
Manabozho 6:31
Mandan 1:49, 2:*28*, 4:5, 53, 9:26, 10:*28–9*, *30*–1
bullboats 2:*48*
dances 8:*44*, 10:*31*
warriors 2:*28*, 8:*44*, 10:42, *46*
Mangas Coloradas (Apache chief) 3:17, 4:39, **6:4**
manifest destiny 6:5
Manitoba 8:38, 43
Manitoba Act (1870) 8:38
Manitou 6:19, 31
Manuelito (Navajo chief) 2:*27*, 50, 7:10, 11
Maricopa 8:11
Marín, Luis 2:60
Marquette, Jacques 2:42, 4:56
marriage 2:39, 3:*4*, 4:54, **6:6–8**, 8:19, 9:27
mixed race *see* Mestizos; Métis; Mulattos; Zambos
Martinez, Maria 6:9, 8:11
Mashpee 8:35
masks 1:47–8, *58*, 3:*15*, **6:10–12**
burial 3:*54*
cornhusk 3:24, *25*
dancing 3:49, *51*, 4:*44*
of the dead 1:*9*, 10, 3:*55*
Mason, John 7:53
Massachusetts Bay colony 7:53
Massasoit 5:33
Maya 1:57, 5:*50*, **6:13–16**
and the afterlife 1:10–*11*
burial ritual masks 6:*11*
cities 6:14–15
dance 3:51
fasting and bloodletting 4:10
gods 6:*15*–16, 7:*30*, 31
and Jaina 5:24
and the Mixtec 6:41
sacred sites 8:54
series of worlds 3:32
see also Bonampak; calendars; Chitchén Itzá; Copán; Palenque; pyramids; Tikal; Uxmal
Mayapán, League of 10:35
Mazariegos, Diego de 2:60
Means, Russell 6:17
medicine 6:18–20
societies *see Midewiwin*
see also sand paintings
medicine bundles 6:*20*, **21–2**, 9:48, 10:8
Medicine Creek Treaty (1854) 10:51
Medicine Lodge Treaty (1867–8) 1:42, 3:21, 5:11
medicine men *see* shamanism
medicine wheels 6:23, 8:55–6
men, effeminate 2:14
Mendota, Treaty of (1851) 5:62
Mendoza, Antonio de 3:26
Menomini 9:46
menstruation 9:47–8
mesa-top villages 4:49, 50, 6:24, 8:18
Mesa Verde 6:24–5
Cliff Palace 1:34, 3:10, 6:*25*
Mescalero Apache 1:36, 2:27
mescaline 7:54
Mesquaki 8:63
Mestizos 6:26
Metacom (Wampanoag chief) 5:33, *34*
metals/metalwork 5:26–7, *30*, 10:7, 14
iron tools 4:44, 10:10
Métis 3:40, 41, **6:27–8**, 8:38, 9:17
see also Red River War; Riel Rebellions
Miami tribe 9:22
Micmac 2:5, 8, 4:9, 6:7, **29–30**, 8:28
***Midewiwin* 6:31–2**, 7:26
migis 6:31–2
migrations
across North America 1:54
and buffalo 3:20, 7:49
see also Bering Bridge
Mikasuki 9:60
Miles, Nelson 3:22, 37, 4:40, 10:*38*
Miller, Al 7:*42*
Mimbreno Apache 3:17, 6:4
Mimbres 6:*47*, *48*, 8:*10*
Minipoka 2:63–4
Minnesota rising (1862) 5:62
missionaries
Catholic 2:*60*, 6:33, *34*–5, *37*, 7:37, 9:6, 59, 60
Presbyterian 7:47
Mission Indians (Californian) 2:45, 3:59, *61*, **6:33–6**, *37*, *38*, 8:*34*
missions 6:37–8
in California *see* Mission Indians
French (Northeast) 4:56, 6:37
Northwest Coast 10:26
Spanish (Florida/Southeast) 9:60
Spanish (Southwest) 4:50, 7:46, 8:18, *24*, 9:38
Mississippians 2:41, **6:39–40**, 8:10, 9:34
decline 1:13, 6:40
farming 1:12–13, 14
see also Cahokia (city); Mound Spiro; Natchez
Mitla (city-state) **6:41**
mixed races
see Mestizos; Métis; Mulattos; Zambos
Mixtec 5:*25*, 6:52
see also Mitla
moccasin game 4:33, *34*
moccasins 1:*61*, 3:*12*, 22, 6:*49*, 10:41–2, *56*
Modoc 1:62, 5:43, **6:42–4**, 8:29
Modoc War 6:*43*, 44, **45–6**
Mogollon 1:15, 34, 2:4, **6:47–8**, 8:10, 47, 9:37, 64, 10:62
Mohave 8:11, 29
Mohawk 4:30, 5:32, 34, **6:49**
language 5:19
and the Revolutionary War 1:32, 2:*31*, 6:49
tribal conflicts 1:20, 4:64, 6:30, 49
see also Brant, Joseph
Mohegan 6:50–1
money, shell 2:45, 4:61, 5:25–6
Montagnais 7:4–5
Monte Alban 6:52
Montezuma II 1:58, 59, 3:28, 9:41, 56
Morley, Sylvanus 5:24
Mormons 7:38, 10:39
Mormon Trail 10:39
Morning Star 2:*61*, 3:30, *43*, 10:5, 27
Mound Builders 9:34
Mound City 6:53–4
mounds 8:55
at Cahokia 2:*42–3*, 6:39, 8:25, *26*, 54–5
Natchez 7:6
see also burial mounds; Serpent Mound
Mound Spiro 6:55

Moundsville **8**:54–5
Mountain People
see Mogollon
mountains, sacred sites **2**:*15*, **8**:*54*, 55
Mounties **1**:17, **3**:41, 47
Mourning Dove **5**:*57*
movies **6**:17, **56–9**, **9**:57
Mulattos **6**:26
Mummy Cave **2**:50
Munsee **3**:56
music **6**:**60–1**
Muskogean speakers **6**:**62–4**
see also Five Civilized Tribes; Natchez
Muskogee *see* Creek
Mysterious One **6**:19

N
Nakota (Yankton) Sioux **9**:26, 27
names **2**:10–11, 12, 62
namimas **5**:44–5
Narragansett **5**:33, 34, 49, **6**:51
Naskapi **2**:5, **7**:**4–5**
Natchez **1**:13, 16, **4**:23, **6**:40, **7**:**6–8**, **10**:52
National Congress of American Indians (NCAI) **5**:4, **7**:42–3
National Council of American Indians **10**:33
National Indian Youth Council (NIYC) **7**:43
Native American Church **6**:38, **7**:48, 54, **8**:29
natural world **1**:52–3, **6**:18, **8**:*55*
see also spirits
Navajo **2**:27, 55, **3**:*62*, **7**:**9–12**, **8**:*13*, **9**:39
and Canyon de Chelly **2**:27, 49, 50, **4**:*49*
crafts **7**:12, **8**:11, 22, *22*, *47*, 49, **10**:*54*
homes **4**:*49*, **7**:12
and the Hopi **4**:*50*, 51
language **1**:54, *55*
medicine bundles **6**:22
origin myths **6**:22, **7**:30
origins **1**:54
religion **6**:22, **7**:30, *31*
reservations **2**:27, 50, **7**:9, *10*, 11, **8**:42
sand paintings **7**:12, **8**:61–2
and silver **5**:27
taboos **9**:48
warriors **4**:12
weddings **6**:*8*
NCAI *see* National Congress of American Indians
necklaces, shell **2**:*45*, **4**:*61*
Necotowance **8**:16
New Archangel **8**:*50*, 51
New Echota Treaty (1835) **5**:49, **10**:20
New Mexico Volunteers **2**:27
newspapers, Cherokee **9**:13
Nezahualcoyotl **9**:56
Nez Percé **2**:53, **4**:53, **7**:**13–16**
and alcohol **1**:17
basket-bags **1**:*62*, 63, **3**:24
horses **1**:62, **7**:14
reservations **7**:15, 16, *17*
retreat toward Canada **5**:28, **7**:*17*–18
see also Joseph, Chief
Nez Percé War **7**:16, **17–18**
Nipmuck **5**:33, 34
NIYC *see* National Indian Youth Council
Niza, Marcos de **3**:26
No Flight societies **10**:49
nomads **1**:38–9, **4**:37, 49, 57
Nootka **3**:5, **4**:19, **5**:45, **7**:**19–21**, 22, **10**:*13*
North, Frank, scouts **9**:*5*
Northwest Coast
blankets **8**:48, *49*
body adornment **2**:23–4
and Californian tribes **2**:46
candlefish **4**:28
canoes **2**:47–8
clothing **3**:14
and copper **5**:26
death customs **3**:54
fishing **4**:18–*19*, 20, 27, **8**:59
homes **4**:47–8
masks **6**:*12*
missions **6**:37–8
music **6**:60
shamans **9**:*47*
taboos **9**:48
tribes *see* Coast Salish; Haida; Kwakiutl; Nootka; Tlingit; Tsimshian
see also potlatches; totem poles
Northwest Fur Company **3**:5, **4**:56
Northwest Mounted Police **6**:*27*
nose rings **2**:23
Nuu-Chah-Nulth *see* Nootka

O
Oakes, Richard **7**:*42*
Oglethorpe, James **5**:32
oil **7**:34
Ojibway (Chippewa) **3**:41, **7**:**24–6**, **9**:22, **10**:58
and bark **2**:8, 9, **7**:24, **10**:*57*
crafts **7**:25, **8**:28, 29
fishing **4**:*18*
fur trade **1**:23, **4**:56, **7**:26
Midewiwin **6**:31, *32*, **7**:26
movie depicting **6**:57
picture writing **1**:*24*
and Pontiac's War **7**:63–4
sweat lodges **9**:46
tribal conflicts **1**:23, **2**:56, **5**:31, **7**:26, **8**:64
see also Erdrich, Louise
Oklahoma **5**:7
see also Indian Territory
Olmec **6**:13–14, **7**:**27–9**
at La Venta **5**:50–1, **7**:*29*
at Monte Alban **6**:52
Olympics
Eskimo **4**:*36*
and Jim Thorpe **9**:57
Omaha tribe, facepaint **2**:*21*
Oñate, Juan de **1**:5, **8**:23, **9**:41
One Bull **5**:*60*
Oneida **1**:20, 32, 33, **2**:*31*
Onondaga **1**:32, **2**:*31*, **10**:40
Opechancano **8**:16
Oregon Trail **3**:5, **5**:9, **6**:*5*, **7**:57, **10**:*39*
orenda **5**:21, 22, **6**:19, **10**:9
Orenda-Manitou **3**:33
origin myths **6**:22, 60, **7**:**30–1**, 32, **10**:54
Oriskany, Battle of **1**:32
ornaments **5**:*24*, **10**:*14*
see also jewelry
Osage **2**:40, **4**:*52*, **7**:**32–4**
Osceola (Seminole chief) **7**:**35**, **9**:9, 12
O'Sullivan, John L. **6**:5
Otomi **4**:4
Ottawa **4**:30, **7**:63, **9**:22, 46
otters **6**:31
ovens **4**:28, **9**:*52*

P
Pacal (Mayan ruler) **6**:15, **7**:39, *40*, **8**:26
paintings
body adornment **2**:*21*, 22, *24*, **3**:*39*, 49–50, **7**:21
on clothing **1**:*40*
on pottery **6**:*14*, *47*, *48*
on rock **1**:*34*, **3**:*7*
sand **2**:45, **7**:12, **8**:61–2
on skin/hide **5**:*16*, 39, *56*, **9**:*28*
wall **1**:*48*, **2**:*4*, 25–*6*
see also petroglyphs
Paiute **1**:62, **8**:29, **10**:34
homes **4**:49, **7**:36
Palacio, Diego García de **3**:23
Palenque **6**:*11*, 14–*15*, **7**:**39–40**, **8**:26
Paleo-Indians **3**:11, **4**:*25*, 59
hunter-gatherers **1**:12, **4**:37, *57*
see also Bering Bridge
Palouse **1**:62, **4**:53
Pamlico **1**:*23*
Pan-Indian Movement **6**:38, **7**:**41–4**
Papago and Pima **1**:16, **2**:53, **4**:46, **7**:**45–7**, **9**:38–9
and Casa Grande **2**:51
language **10**:34
pottery **8**:11
reservations **7**:47, **8**:42
symbolic scalping **9**:4
taboos **9**:49
parfleches **7**:14
Paris, Treaty of (1763) **4**:30
Parker, Cynthia Ann **7**:48
Parker, Ely **2**:*35*, 37
Parker, Quanah **3**:22, **5**:39, **6**:38, **7**:**48**, 54
passports **5**:53
Pawnee **2**:*41*, **7**:**49–51**
and buffalo **2**:33, **7**:49
children **2**:*61*, **7**:51
cosmology **3**:31
scouts **9**:*5*
tribal bundles **6**:22, **7**:50
Payne's Landing, Treaty of (1832) **7**:35, **9**:11
Peltier, Leonard **7**:44, **9**:44
pemmican **4**:28
Penn, William **3**:*57*, 58, **10**:*19*, 40
Penobscot **2**:9, **8**:29
Pequot **6**:50–1, **7**:52, 53
Pequot War **6**:51, **7**:**52–3**
pestles **9**:*14*
petroglyphs **7**:*23*, **8**:56
peyote **7**:**54**
see also religion, peyote
picture writing/pictographs **1**:*24*, **5**:*56*
see also paintings
Pilgrims **6**:51, **9**:*16*
Pima *see* Papago and Pima
piñon nuts **7**:36, 37
pipes **7**:*34*, **9**:*14*, 28–9, *49*, 64
tomahawk-pipe **10**:*7*
Pitt, William **4**:30
Plains tribes **5**:*9*, **7**:**55–7**
and the afterlife **1**:*9–10*
birth ceremonies **2**:10
boats **2**:48
body paints **2**:22, **10**:*46*
and cattle trails **2**:53
and the Civil War **1**:27
clothing **1**:47, **3**:11
crafts **1**:46, 47, **8**:*29*
death customs **1**:*10*, **3**:52, 54, 55
education **3**:62
firearms **4**:16, *17*
food **4**:28
gambling **4**:33
homes **2**:*56*, **3**:*20*, **4**:47, *48*, 49
hunting **4**:27
language **7**:56
medicine necklaces **6**:*19*
and the railroads **8**:31–2
religion **7**:56–7, **9**:*44*
rites of passage **4**:11
shields **9**:*24*, *25*
tribes *see* Arapaho; Assiniboine; Blackfoot; Cheyenne; Comanche; Crow; Kiowa; Pawnee; Sioux
war costumes **10**:41–2
warriors **4**:12–13, 16, *17*, **7**:*49*, **9**:*24*, **10**:*45*, *46*
women **10**:52–3
see also buffalo; counting coup; horses; Indian Wars; medicine wheels; movies Sun Dance
Plains Wars *see* Indian Wars
Plateau groups *see* Basin and Plateau
Pocahontas **6**:57, **7**:**58–9**, **8**:15, 16
poets **5**:56
polygamy **6**:8
Pomo **2**:46, **4**:15, **6**:37, **7**:**60**
basketry **1**:*63*, **7**:*60*
and the Russians **8**:51
Ponce de León, Juan **9**:35, 41, 59
Pontiac (Ottawa chief) **1**:24, **4**:30, **6**:20, **7**:**61–2**
Pontiac's War **1**:24, **2**:30, **4**:6, 17, 30, **7**:26, 62, **63–4**, **10**:40
treaty ending **10**:*21*
Popé **4**:53, **8**:*23*–4
population density **6**:36, **8**:**4–5**
Popul Vuh (book) **7**:31
Port Elliot Treaty (1855) **9**:6
Potawatomi **9**:22, 46
potlatches **1**:52, **3**:*55*, **4**:*44*, **7**:23, **8**:**6–8**, **9**:62, **10**:11, 25
pottery **8**:**9–11**
Acoma **1**:*4*, **8**:10
Anasazi **1**:34, *35*, **2**:*50*
Caddo **2**:*39*

Hohokam **4**:*46*
and Maria Martinez **6**:9, **8**:11
Mayan **6**:*14*
Mississippian **6**:*39*, *40*
Mogollon **6**:*47*, *48*
Pueblo **8**:*10*–11, 20
Poundmaker (chief) **3**:41, **8**:43
poverty, **1**:*25*, **8**:**12–14**
Powamuy **8**:45
power, medicine **6**:19–20
Powhatan (Algonquian chief) **7**:58, **8**:**15**, 16
Powhatan tribes **1**:*21*, **2**:23, **8**:16, **9**:17
Powhatan Wars 8:**16**
powwows **6**:30, **7**:*16*
prayer sticks **4**:14
Presbyterians **7**:47
Proclamation Line **8**:40, **9**:17, **10**:38–9
Próclamation of 1763 **7**:64
Prophet, the (Tenskwatawa) **9**:53, 54
puberty **1**:40, **2**:12, **8**:46
Pueblo (tribes) **1**:6, **5**:47, **8**:**17–20**, **9**:37–8, 39
art and crafts **1**:46, *48*, **8**:*10*–11, 20, 48–9
casinos **5**:*54*
clans **3**:8–9
clothing **3**:11, **8**:*20*
dance **3**:50, **4**:14, **6**:26
drums **6**:60
Eastern and Western **8**:17, **9**:38
farming **1**:*14*, 15, **8**:20
and feathers **4**:14–15
horses **4**:53
language groups **9**:38, 50
Martinez, Maria **6**:9, **8**:11
masks **6**:12
music **6**:61
religion **6**:38, **8**:18, 20
series of worlds **3**:31
villages **8**:19–20
see also Acoma; Cliff Palace; Hopi; kachinas; *kivas*; Southwest tribes; Zuni
Pueblo Bonito 2:*55*, **8**:**21–2**
Pueblo Rebellion 1:5, 6, **4**:50, 53, **6**:20, **8**:18, **23–4**, **10**:62
pueblos (buildings) **1**:4, **4**:49, **6**:48, **9**:*38*, 52
see also Acoma village; Chaco Canyon; Taos
Puritans **6**:37
Pyramid Lake **10**:51
pyramids 8:**25–6**
at El Tajín **3**:*32*, **4**:4, **8**:26
at Teotihuacan **8**:*25*, 26, 54, **10**:*5*
at Tula **10**:*4*, **6**, *27*
Mayan **3**:*6*, *23*, **6**:*13*, 15, **7**:40, **8**:26, **9**:*58*, **10**:35
Olmec **5**:50
see also mounds

Q

Quebec **5**:35, *36*, **6**:37
Queen Anne's War 8:**27**
Quetzalcoatl (god) **1**:57, **3**:6, **4**:*28*, **9**:56, **10**:5
Quetzalcoatl (warrior) **10**:5, 27
Quiche **6**:13, **10**:6
Quigualtam **7**:6
quillwork 1:*22*, **6**:*29*, *30*, *50*, *51*, **8**:**28–9**
and beadwork 3:22, **4**:*17*, **7**:*56*, *57*, **8**:28–*9*, **10**:*13*, 14
Quivira 8:**30**

R

races **3**:*9*, **4**:36
Radisson, Pierre **4**:55
raiding **1**:39, **10**:47
see also horses
railroads 1:30, **3**:41, **4**:*8*, 51, **8**:**31–2**
and the buffalo **2**:34, **8**:*31*–2
rain
dances **3**:50, **4**:4, 14, **10**:*62*
rain kachinas **5**:29
rituals/ceremonies **1**:16, **7**:46
songs for **6**:60
Raleigh, Walter **9**:63
rasps **6**:61
rattles **3**:48, **6**:60–1, **9**:*21*
Raven, trickster **7**:*22*, 23
Reagan, Ronald **8**:*14*
recognition 8:**33–5**
Red Cloud (Sioux chief) **5**:11, **12**, **8**:**36**, 37, **9**:29, **10**:60
Red Cloud's War 3:36, **8**:**37**, **9**:29–30
Red Power **7**:43
Red River War 7:48, **8**:**38**
Red Sticks **10**:44
Red Tomahawk **9**:*27*
reincarnation **1**:9, 52
religion **3**:31–2
Aztec **1**:57–8, *59*
Blackfoot **2**:16–17
Christianity **3**:59, 62, **5**:34, **6**:26, **9**:21, *44*, **10**:9
Crow **3**:43–4
Iroquois **5**:21–2, 63–4
longhouse religion **5**:63–4
Mayan **7**:31
Pan-Indian **6**:38
peyote (Native American Church) **5**:39, **6**:38, **7**:48, 54, **8**:29
Pueblo **6**:38, **8**:18, 20
secret cults **10**:63–4
and totem poles **10**:11
see also afterlife; cosmology; Ghost Dance; gods; missions; spirits
relocation **8**:4
see also disenfranchisement; reservations
Reno, Marcus **5**:*59*
reservations 1:24, 37, **8**:*4*, **39–42**
and alcohol **1**:17
Bosque Redondo **2**:27, 50, **7**:11
and the Bureau of Indian Affairs **2**:35–6, *37*
for Californian tribes **6**:36
divided up *see* Allotment Act
gambling in **4**:34
membership of **5**:52
poverty **8**:13
schools **2**:*36*, **3**:64
see also Indian Territory
Riel Rebellions 3:47, **6**:28, **8**:38, **43**
rituals 6:19, **8**:**44–6**
and alcohol **1**:16
Apache **1**:39–40
before Vision Quest **10**:36
bloodletting **4**:10, 11
and buffalo *see* buffalo
corn **3**:25
death **3**:54, 55, **7**:7
fishing **4**:18–19
hunting **1**:44, 60–1, **3**:53, **4**:*59*, **7**:5, 20
and lacrosse **5**:46
longhouse religion **5**:63–4
and masks **6**:10–12
salmon **8**:59
see also ceremonies; dance; Ghost Dance; masks; sacrifice; scalping; Sun Dance; Vision Quest
Road Man **7**:54
roads *see* highways
Rogers, Robert **7**:61
Rolfe, John **7**:**58**, *59*, **8**:15
Roman Nose **5**:10–11
Rosebud, Battle of the **5**:12, 59
Ross, John (Cherokee chief) **1**:*28*–9, **10**:*16*
Rowlandson, Mary **5**:34
rugs and blankets 7:*12*, *33*, **8**:**47–9**, **9**:62, **10**:*54*
infected with smallpox **7**:64
Ruiz, Samuel **2**:60
Rupert's Land **8**:38
Russians
missions **6**:37–8
trade **8**:50–1, **9**:61, **10**:13
Russia, Wars with 8:**50–1**

S

Sacajawea 7:*15*, **8**:**52–3**
Sacred Bundles **7**:50
sacred circles
see medicine wheels
sacred sites 2:*15*, **8**:**54–6**
see also Bonampak; medicine wheels; mounds
sacrifice, human
Aztec **1**:57–8, **3**:51, **8**:*45*
Mayan **7**:31
Mississippian **6**:40
Natchez **7**:7
Sa-Ga-Yeath-Qua-Pieth-Tow (Iroquois chief) **5**:*20*
St. Augustine **9**:*11*, 16, 41
St. Michael (trading post) **8**:51
SAI (Society of American Indians) **7**:41, 42
Salado **2**:51
Salish 8:**57–8**
see also Coast Salish
salmon 8:**6**
see also fishing
Sand Creek Massacre 1:41–2, **2**:*57*, 59, **5**:10, **8**:**60**
sand paintings 2:45, **7**:12, **8**:**61–2**
Santa Barbara **8**:*34*
Santa Fe **8**:23, 24, **9**:16
Santa Fe Trail **3**:27, **5**:9
Santee
see Dakota (Santee) Sioux
Saratoga, Battle of **1**:32
Sarcee, origins **1**:54
Sassacus (Pequot chief) **6**:51
Satana (White Bear; Kiowa chief) **5**:38
Sauk and Fox 8:**63–4**
Black Hawk's War **2**:18, **8**:*64*
death rituals **3**:55
and elm bark **2**:8, **8**:*63*
homes **4**:49, **8**:*63*
tribal conflicts **7**:26, **8**:*64*
Scalp Dance **3**:*49*
scalping 2:5, **3**:*43*, 53, **5**:*11*, **9**:**4**, 28, **10**:*47*
and the Blackfoot **2**:15
and the American Revolutionary War **1**:33
scalp shirts **10**:41
Schoolcraft, Henry **4**:45
scouts 9:**5**, **10**:42
seals **4**:19
Seattle, Chief 5:13, **9**:**6**
Segard, Gabriel **4**:*62*
self-determination **2**:37
Seminole 4:9, 21, **7**:35, **9**:**7–10**, 36, 60, **10**:*55*
and the American Civil War **1**:28
homes **4**:48–9
origins **6**:*64*, **7**:35, **9**:7, 36
and runaway African slaves **9**:7, 11
see also Osceola; Seminole Wars
Seminole Wars 7:35, **9**:8, 9, 10, **11–12**
Seneca **1**:32, **2**:*31*, **7**:63, **10**:40
Sequoyah 4:24, **9**:**13**
Seri **2**:45
Serpent Mound 1:*7*, 8, **8**:54, 56, **9**:**14–15**
Serra, Junipero **6**:*34*–5
settlers 8:*12*, **9**:**16–18**
introducing alcohol **1**:16–17
manifest destiny **6**:5
and Native-American land **5**:*5*, *6*–7, 8, **8**:12
westward expansion **1**:37, **6**:5, **9**:*17*–18, **10**:38–9
see also cattle trails; epidemics; gold prospectors; wagon trails
Seven Cities of Cibola/gold **3**:*26*, 27, **8**:30, **10**:62
Shahaka (Mandan chief) **10**:*29*
shamanism 4:*11*, 41, **6**:18–19, **8**:46, **9**:**19–21**
Apache **1**:39
and the buffalo **2**:33
and Californian tribes **2**:46
Cheyenne **2**:57
Chumash **3**:*7*
clothing **9**:*20*, *47*
Crow **3**:*44*
and European colonists **6**:20
and fasting **4**:*11*
Hopewell **1**:*8*
Iroquois **5**:21
Lenape **3**:57
and sand paintings **8**:61, 62
spirit journeys **1**:9
and sweat lodges **9**:45
and totems **10**:8
Tsimshian **10**:25
and Vision Quest **10**:*36*

women 10:54
Sharitarish (Pawnee chief) 7:*49*
Shawnee 7:63, **9:22–3**
and the American Civil War 1:29
and the American Revolutionary War 1:33, 9:23
and the War of 1812 10:*43*
see also Tecumseh
Shawnee Trail 2:52, *53*
sheep 8:47, 48
shells
shell-money 2:45, 4:61, 5:25–6
spirit-carrying 6:31–2
trade items 10:*13*, *14*
Sherman, William T. 2:27
shields 3:*40*, **9:24–5**, 29
Shoshoni 1:62, 2:17, 7:38, 10:34
silver 5:27, *30*, 7:*11*, 12
sings 7:12
Siouan speakers 9:4, **26**, 10:45
Sioux 2:53, *63*, 4:17, **9:27–30**
bows and arrows 2:*29*
crafts 3:*12*, 7:*57*, 8:29
divisions *see* Dakota (Santee) Sioux; Lakota (Teton) Sioux; Nakota (Yankton) Sioux
Ghost Dance 3:46, 4:*41*, 7:38, 9:30
horses 4:53, 56
lacrosse 5:*46*
land taken from 2:20, 3:37, 46
language 9:26
movies depicting 6:58–9
religion 6:19, 9:28–9
reservations 2:20, 5:*4*, 8:*41*
Sun Dance 3:32, 9:43, *44*
tribal conflicts 2:56, 7:26, 9 *28*
warriors 2:*58*, 4:12–*13*, 9:28, 10:*47*
Woodland and Plains 9:27
see also Black Hills; Crazy Horse; Indian Wars; Little Bighorn, Battle of; Red Cloud's War; Sitting Bull; Wounded Knee
Sitting Bull (Sioux shaman) 4:11, 5:12, 8:36, 37, **9:31–2**, 10:60
and Crowfoot 2:17, 3:47
killed 9:*27*, 30, 32, 10:60
and Little Bighorn 5:12, 58–9, 9:30, 32, 10:*37*
migration to Canada 3:36, 5:61, 9:32
Skidi Pawnee 2:41, 3:*30*
skins, animal 8:47
skulls, buffalo 2:33, *34*, 6:23, 8:*46*
Sky City *see* Acoma Village
slaves 4:61, 5:43, 9:62, 10:25
of the Five Civilized Tribes 4:22
mission Indians as 6:34–5
plantation 1:14
runaway African 9:7, 11
smallpox *see* epidemics
Smith, John 7:58, 8:15
Smohalla Cult 6:38
smoking *see* tobacco
Snake and Antelope ceremony 4:51
Snake Woman 1:57
snow goggles 1:*45*, 5:15
snowshoes 1:*20*, 22, 51, 3:38
Society of American Indians (SAI) 7:41, 42
Solomon Fork, Battle of 5:10
Soloviev, Ivan 8:51
songs 6:60
Soto, Hernando de 6:40, 7:6, *8*, **9:33**, 35, 41, 59–60
soul-catchers 10:25
Southeast/Florida tribes 3:25, 4:9, 19, **9:34–6**
see also Caddo; Cahokia; Five Civilized Tribes; Mississippians; Muskogean speakers; Natchez; Timucua
Southern Arapaho 1:41, 42
Southern Cheyenne 1:42
Southwest tribes 9:37–9
and the Civil War 1:27
crafts 4:14, 8:10–11, 48–9
diet 4:27
homes 4:*49*
ovens 4:28
see also Anasazi; Apache; Cochise; Hohokam; Mogollon; Navajo; Papago and Pima; Pueblo (tribes)
sovereignty 5:52, 8:39, 9:36, 10:19
Spain, wars with/Spanish conquest 1:35, **9:40–1**
and the Acoma 1:5, 6
and the Apache 1:36–7, 9:39
and the Aztecs 1:*57*, 58–9, 3:28–9, 33, 9:41, 56
of Chiapas 2:60
conquistadors *see* Coronado, Francisco de; Cortes, Hernando; Ponce de León, Juan; Soto, Hernando de
and horses 1:36–7, 4:52–3, 9:40
and Mestizos 6:26
and the Navajo 2:50
and Taos pueblo 9:51–2
see also epidemics; missions; Pueblo Rebellion
Spanish Succession, War of the 8:27
spears 4:*25*, 59
Spirit Canoe Dance 3:51
spirits 3:52
Apache 1:*40*
Caddo 2:39
Coast Salish 3:15
Corn Spirits 3:25
and dance 3:50–1
of the dead 1:10–11, 3:54–5, 9:4, 28
Great Spirit 3:33
guardian 4:13, 7:13–14, 9:24, *25*, 10:8, 47
Lenape 3:58
and masks 6:10–11
of the natural world 1:52, 2:13, 3:31, 4:26, *59*, 6:21, 7:23, *37*, 9:24–*5*, 49
Northwest Coast 7:23
and potlatches 8:6
and shamanism 9:20–1
and smoking 9:63, 64
see also kachinas; totemism; Vision Quest
Spirit Singing 3:15
sports
and Jim Thorpe 9:57
see also games
Spotted Tail (chief) 3:46, 8:37
squash 1:12, 14
Squier, Ephraim G. 6:54
Standing Bear (Ponca chief) 9:*26*
Standing Bear, Henry (Sioux chief) 2:20
Stephens, John L. 3:23
sterilization 9:42
Stone John 7:52–3
stories *see* legends/stories
Subarctic tribes 1:45, 2:5
bark 2:8, 9
clothing 3:12
totems 10:9
see also Aleut; Algonquian tribal group; Cree; Micmac
Sullivan, John 1:33, 2:31
Sun, and the Maya 1:11
Sun Dance 2:33, 6:59, 7:56–7, **9:43–4**
banned 3:44, 9:44
Blackfoot 2:14, 16–*17*
Cheyenne 2:56, 58
Kiowa 5:39
lodges 3:32
Sioux 3:32, 9:*43*, *44*
sweat lodges 6:43, 8:46, **9:45–6**
Sxwaixwe, masks 3:*15*

T

taboos 9:47–9
Taensa 6:64
Tanoan speakers 9:50, 10:34
Taos pueblo 8:17, 18–19, 9:*38*, **51–2**
tattoos 2:*22*, 3:12, *39*, 40, *41*, 9:*60*, 10:47
Taylor, Zachary 9:12
Tecumseh 2:18, 6:20, 7:26, 9:23, **53–4**, 10:43, 44
teeth, filed 2:23
Temple Mound Builders *see* Mississippians
temples 2:*25*, 41
Tenochtitlán 1:56, 59, 3:28, 29, 9:41, **55–6**
Tenskwatawa 9:*22*, *23*, 53, 54
Teotihuacan 8:*25*, 26, 54, 10:4, *5*
tepees 1:14, 39, *41*, 4:47, *48*, *49*, 8:*40*, 9:26, 10:*50*
facing the sun 3:31
and the travois 10:18
villages 1:*50*, 2:*56*, 3:*20*, 5 *37*
Tequesta 9:59
Terry Alfred 5:59
Teton Sioux *see* Lakota (Teton) Sioux
Texas 5:8, 9
textiles 8:47–8
Thames, Battle of the 9:23, 54, 10:44
Thayendanegea *see* Brant, Joseph
Thorpe, Jim 9:57
Three Affiliated Tribes 10:31
Three Fires Confederacy 2:9
thunderbirds 1:*42*, 4:*42*, *44*, 10:*8*
Tiguex 3:*27*, 8:30
Tikal 9:58
Timucua 3:12, **9:59–60**
body adornment 2:22–3, 5:25, 9:*60*
Tipai 6:34, 35
Tippecanoe, Battle of (1811) 9:*22*, *23*
tiswin 1:16
Tlaloc 1:57
Tlaxcala (city) 4:10
Tlaxcala (people) 3:28
Tlingit 6:37–8, 8:*6*, 48, *51*, 59, **9:61–2**, 10:*42*
Chilkat blankets 8:*48*, 9:62, 10:24
and the Russians 8:*50*, 51, 9:*61*
and trade 7:21, 8:51, 9:61, 10:12
tobacco 1:14, **9:63–4**, 10:36
ceremonies 3:44, 9:63
and the Europeans 1:14, 9:17, 63
see also pipes
tobogganing 4:36
Tollan *see* Tula
Tolowa 3:50
Toltec 3:6, 8:22, **10:4–6**
see also Teotihuacan; Tula
tomahawks 10:7
tools, iron 4:44, 10:10
Topiltzin *see* Quetzalcoatl (warrior)
totemism 4:48, **10:8–9**
totem poles 3:*8*, 4:*43*, 7:21, 10:*8*, 9, **10–11**, *11*
raising 10:*23*, *24*
tools for 10:14
Totonac 4:4
Tovar, Pedro de 3:27
Toypurina 6:35
trade 1:49, **10:12–14**
across the Plains 7:56
alcohol 1:*16*–17
in California 2:44–5
and the Chinook 3:4–5
feathers 4:15
guns 2:*14*, 4:17, 10:13–14
horses 4:53, 10:14
metals 5:26–7, 10:14, 26
see also fur trade
trading posts 1:*16*, *17*, 5:*30*, 7:*10*, 10:14
Trail of Broken Treaties march (1972) 6:17, 7:44, 10:22
trails *see* cattle trails; wagon trails
Trail of Tears 9:9, 36, **10:15–16**, 21, 58
travois 2:15, 6:23, 7:*55*, **10:17–18**
treaties 1:30, 3:60, 4:20, 8:40, 41, 9:17–18, **10:19–22**
false/fraudulent 1:17, 9:17, 10:20
and firearms 4:17

and the Allotment Act (1887) **1**:25–6
nonrepresentative **5**:48–9, **9**:17, **10**:20
and tribal recognition **8**:34
and water rights **10**:50
see also land rights
Treaty 7 **3**:47
tribes
brotherhoods **7**:23
extinction **4**:8–9
formation **4**:59
as nations **5**:52
recognition **8**:33–5
societies **10**:30–1
Trickster **5**:56, **10**:54
tsetseka **8**:6, 59
Tsimshian 3:*51*, **10:23–6**
Tuekakas **7**:15
Tula 10:4–5, 6, **27**
tule reed **2**:48, **6**:*42*
turkeys **4**:15, 27
turtles **2**:*10*
Tuscarora, and the Revolutionary War **1**:32, **2**:*31*

U

umiaks **1**:44, **4**:60, **5**:*16*
Unalactigo **3**:56
Unami **3**:56
Uncas (Pequot chief) **6**:51, **7**:53
Union of New Brunswick Indians **6**:30
Union of Nova Scotia Indians **6**:30
Upper Missouri tribes 10:28–31
see also Arikara; Hidatsa; Mandan
urban life 6:49, **8**:13–14, **10:32–3**
Ute **1**:62, **8**:47, **10**:34
Uto-Aztecan 9:50, **10:34**
Utrecht, Treaty of (1713) **8**:27
Uxmal 6:*13*, 41, **10:35**

V

Vancouver, George **5**:*45*
Vargas, Diego de **8**:24
Velázquez, Diego **3**:28
Verrazano, Giovanni da **3**:58
Victorio **4**:39
Viikita ceremony **7**:46
Vikings **5**:17
violins **6**:61
Virginia **5**:47, **9**:17, *63*
Vision Quest 2:13, 57–8, **3**:43–4, 62, **4**:11, **8**:46, **9**:29, **10:36–7**
visions *see* dreams and visions
Vizenor, Gerald **7**:26
voting rights **5**:4, *52*, **7**:42
voyageurs **7**:26

W

Wagon Box Fight **3**:36, **8**:*37*
wagon trails 5:9, **6**:44, **9**:*18*, **10:38–9**
see also Bozeman Trail; Oregon Trail; Santa Fe Trail
Wakonda **6**:19
Wampanoag **5**:*33*, 34, 49, **6**:51
Mashpee **8**:35
wampum 4:45, **10:40**
belts **5**:*19*, 22, **26**, **10**:*40*
war bonnets **4**:*12*, *13*, **10**:42
war costumes 2:*16*, **3**:*17*, *42*, **8**:*51*, **10:41–2**
paints **2**:22, **10**:42, *46*
see also feathers
warfare **4**:33
War of 1812 4:24, **9**:11, **10:43–4**
and Tecumseh **9**:*53*, 54, **10**:43, 44
war parties, Apache **1**:39
warriors 2:*28*, **4**:11, **10:45–7**
Apache **3**:*16*, *17*, **4**:12
body adornment **2**:*21*, *22*, **10**:42, *46*, 47
Cheyenne **2**:57, *58*
clothing *see* war costumes
feathers for 3:*17*, **4:12–13**, **9**:*24*
Osage **7**:*32*, *34*
Sioux **2**:*58*, **4**:12–*13*, **9**:28
totems of **10**:8–9
see also counting coup; scalping; shields; warrior societies
warrior societies 10:48–9
Blackfoot **2**:14–15, **10**:48
Cheyenne **2**:57
Wars for the West *see* Indian Wars
Washington, George **2**:31, **4**:29
Washo **9**:48
water
rights 7:47, **10:50–1**
sacred sites **8**:54–6
storage **1**:35
see also irrigation
Watie, Stand (Cherokee chief) **1**:28, *29*, 30
Wayne, Anthony **3**:*58*, **9**:53
weaving **7**:12, 37, **8**:47–9, **10**:*54*
Western Apache **1**:36, *37*, 40
Western Cattle Trail **2**:52, *53*
West, Joseph **6**:4
West, Sir Thomas **3**:56
whale hunting **4**:19, 20, 60, **7**:*19*–20
Wheeler-Howard Act *see* Indian Reorganization Act
wheels **10**:17
see also medicine wheels
White Bull (Sioux shaman) **10**:*36*
White Cloud (the Winnebago Prophet) **2**:18, **8**:64
White Painted Woman **1**:40, **8**:46
Wichita (tribe) 2:41, **7**:51, **8**:30
wickiups **1**:39, **2**:*44*, **4**:49, **7**:36, *60*
wigwams **1**:*19*, *23*, **2**:8, **4**:47, **6**:29, **7**:*4*
Wi-Jun-Jon (Assiniboine chief) **1**:*49*
Wilderness, Battle of the **7**:61
wild rice **4**:*27*, 58, **7**:25
William III, king of Britain **5**:*35*
Wilson's Creek, Battle of **1**:28, *29*
windigos **6**:19
Winnebago **1**:*46*, **8**:29
Winnebago Prophet (White Cloud) **2**:18, **8**:64
Winnemucca, Sarah **10**:*52*
Winter's Doctrine **10**:50–1
Withlacoochee, Battle of **9**:9
Wolf Dance **7**:*21*
Wolfe, James **4**:*30*
Wolf Mountain, Battle of **5**:61
wolves **10**:9
women 2:62, **10:52–5**
Apache **1**:38
clothing **3**:*4*, 12, **4**:*24*
games **4**:36
Huron **4**:63
menstruating **9**:47–8
Natchez **7**:*6*
puberty **1**:40, **8**:46
societies **10**:31
tattoos and body paint **2**:22, **9**:*60*
see also birth customs; marriage
woodcarving **10**:11, 14, 24
Woodland tribes 9:26, 34, **10:56–8**
and bark **2**:*8*, *9*
and birth **2**:10, 11, **9**:48
clothing **3**:14
diet **4**:19, 27
homes **4**:48
language **2**:41, **9**:26
totems **10**:9
see also Adena and Hopewell; Delaware; Huron; Iroquois; Sauk and Fox
wool **8**:47
worlds, series of **3**:31–2
World War II **5**:4, **7**:11, 47
Wounded Knee
massacre **1**:42, 61, **4**:*41*, 42, **5**:12, **7**:38, *41*, **8**:32, **9**:30, **10:59–60**, 61
occupation of (1973) **6**:17, **7**:44, **9**:30
Wovoka 1:61, **4**:41–2, **7**:38, **9**:32, **10**:59, **61**
Wright, Ben **6**:44
writing
Cherokee language **9**:13
Olmec hieroglyphs **7**:28
see also picture writing/pictographs
Wyandots/Wyandottes **4**:64
Wyoming Valley Massacre **1**:33

X

Xiu **10**:35

Y

Yahola, Opothle (Creek chief) **1**:29
Yakima **5**:5
Yamasee **9**:60
Yankton *see* Nakota (Yankton) Sioux
Yaqui **6**:26, **10**:34
Yellow Calf (chief) **4**:*12*
Yellowtail, Thomas **3**:33
Yokuts **2**:46, **3**:48
Yuma **6**:61, **8**:11
Yupiks **1**:43, **5**:18
Yurok **2**:46, **4**:15, **7**:30–1

Z

Zaldivar, Juan de **1**:5
Zambos **6**:26
Zapatista National Liberation Army **2**:60
Zapotec **6**:41, 52
Zia tribe **9**:*37*
Ziolkowski, Korczak **2**:20
Zuni 1:6, 36, **3**:*52*, **5**:*27*, **8**:10, 17, **10:62–4**
featherwork **4**:14, **10**:*64*
and Francisco de Coronado **3**:26, 27, **8**:30, **10**:62
and the Mogollon **6**:48

ACKNOWLEDGMENTS

Picture Credits

Bridgeman Art Library: Art Gallery of Ontario 56b; Brown Partworks: National Archives 36; Corbis: 18, Tom Bean 8, 11, Bettmann 32, 38, 50, Francis G. Mayer 19, Progessive Image 23, 24, M. T. Sedam 51; Hulton-Getty Picture Library: 5; Mary Evans Picture Library: 37; Peter Newark Historical Pictures: 1, 4, 7, 15, 16, 17, 22, 29, 31, 43, 46tl, 47, 52, 53, 54, 55, 57tr, 59, 60, 61, 62; Northwind Picture Archive: 21, 39, 44, 45; N. J. Saunders: 10; Sylvia Bancroft Hunt Pictures: 20, 28, 40, 42, 46br, 48, 49, 56tr, 57br, 63, 64; Werner Forman Archive: 9, 12, 13, 14, 25, 27, 35, 41.

Text Contributors

Norman Bancroft Hunt, Steven L. Grafe, Ray Granger, Jen Green, Charlotte Greig, Casey Horton, Chris Marshall, Nigel Ritchie, Antony Shaw, Stephen Small, Donald Sommerville, Chris Westhorp.

Do you know?

When things get hot or cold, they change. Look what happens to water!

When water gets very cold, it turns to ice and snow.

When water gets very hot, it boils. It turns to steam.

Here are some hot and cold things.

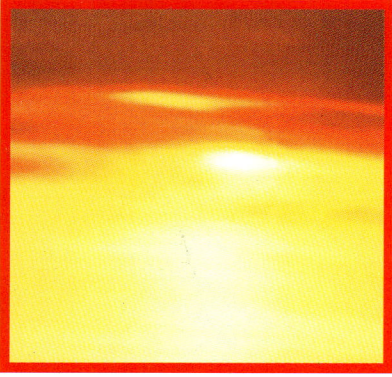

Ice lolly

Desert

Fire

Pool

Sun

Can you write a story with these words?

Here are some words about heat.

Hot

Cold

Warm

Cool

Icy

Sonya and Greg sit under a tree.
Here it is not too hot and not
too cold.

It is just right!

Just right

What a day! The sun was hot,
then the penguin house was cold.

The rainforest was warm and damp,
then the wind was cool and dry.

The wind makes things dry, too.

These towels are drying in the wind.

Wind

What is cool and dry?

The wind blows and makes
Sonya and Greg feel cool.
Inside, a fan makes a wind!

Some animals like hot places, and some like cold places.

Greg and Sonya want to see them all!

Hot

What is hot?

Today the sun is hot.
Sonya and Greg stand in the sun.
It makes them feel hot, too.

The sun is too hot for Sonya,
but not for the camels.

Camels live in a desert.
They stand in the sun all day.

Cold

What is cold?

Splash! That water is cold.
It makes Greg shiver.
But the seals love it!

If you jump in the sea on a hot day, it feels very cold!

Getting warm

What is warm?

Warm is a little hot.

Greg sits in the sun to get warm.

So does a crocodile!

In winter, this fox has fur to keep it warm. Greg and Sonya have winter coats to keep them warm.

Staying cool

What is cool?

Cool is a little cold.
When hippos get too warm,
they cool off in the water.

You can swim in a pool
to stay cool, too!

Fire

What is very hot?

Fire is very hot. Sonya and Greg eat hot dogs cooked on a fire.

Warm and damp

The rainforest hall is warm and damp.

Water drips from the trees and flowers. Bright birds call.

Soon Sonya and Greg feel warm and damp, too.

The penguin house is very cold. Penguins live on the ice. They swim in the icy water. Brrrr!

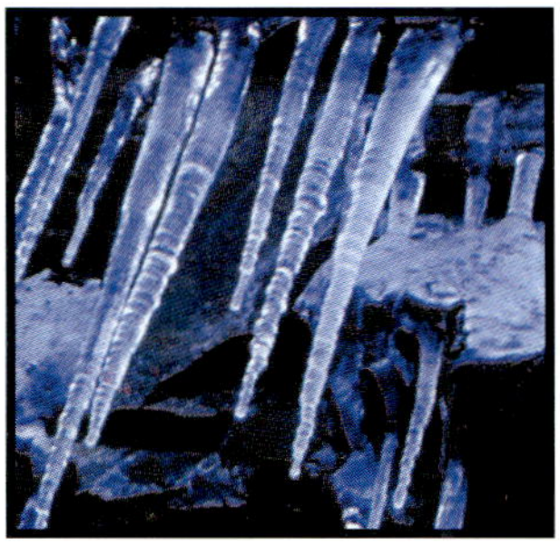

Ice

What is very cold?

When water gets very cold, it turns to ice. When ice gets warm, it turns to water!

When rocks get very,
very hot, they melt.
They glow like fire!

Hot and cold

Sonya and Greg go to see the animals at the park.

READING ABOUT

Hot and Cold

By Jim Pipe

Aladdin/Watts
London • Sydney